GW00356671

Essential
Belgium
(Flanders Region)

by Jeroen van der Spek

For many years now, Flanders has
been the favourite travel destination of
journalist Jeroen van der Spek. He has
travelled across the region at regular
intervals in search of the best pubs and
the most atmospheric towns. He has
also written a travel guide to Antwerp,
and has published widely on travel,
lifestyle and the Internet. His guides
are characterised by a lively interest in
history and a great love of the
Burgundian way of life.

Above: Antwerp, seen from the left bank

AA Publishing

The Flemish lion on the official Flemish flag

Front cover: *Schellemolen Windmill; Bruges boat trips; Fraikin sculpture*
Back cover: *Flemish Mussels*

Author: Jeroen van der Spek
Translated from the Dutch by: Aletta Stevens
© 2000 Kosmos-Z&K Uitgevers B.V., Utrecht
Typesetting: Studio Imago,
Jacqueline Bronsema, Amersfoort
© Automobile Association Developments Limited 2000,
© Maps: Bert Stamkot, Cartografisch Bureau MAP,
Amsterdam
First edition

English language edition produced for AA Publishing by:
g-and-w PUBLISHING, Oxfordshire, UK

A CIP catalogue record for this book is available from the
British Library
ISBN 0 7495 3192 4

Kosmos-Z&K publishers make every effort to ensure that
their travel guides are as up-to-date as possible.
Circumstances, however, are very changeable. Opening
times and prices change, and roads are built or closed.
Therefore, Kosmos-Z&K publishers do not accept liability for
any incorrect or obsolete information. Assessments of
attractions, hotels, restaurants and so forth are based upon
the author's own experience and, therefore, descriptions
given in this guide necessarily contain an element of
subjective opinion which may not reflect the publisher's
opinion or dictate a reader's own experience on another
occasion.
  We have tried to ensure accuracy in this guide, but
things do change and we would be grateful if readers
would advise us of any inaccuracies they may encounter.

English language edition published by AA Publishing, a
trading name of Automobile Association Developments
Limited, whose registered office is Norfolk House,
Priestley Road, Basingstoke, Hampshire, RG24 9NY.
Registered number 1878835.

Printed and bound in Italy by Printer Trento srl

Find out more about
AA Publishing and the
wide range of services
the AA provides by visit-
ing our web site at
www.theAA.com

Contents

About this Book

Essential _Flanders_ is divided into five sections to cover the most important aspects of your visit to Flanders.

Viewing Flanders pages 5–14
    An introduction to Flanders by the author
    Flanders's Features
    Essence of Flanders
    The Shaping of Flanders
    Peace and Quiet
    Flanders's Famous

Top Ten pages 15–26
The author's choice of the Top Ten places to see in Flanders, listed in alphabetical order, each with practical information.

What to See pages 27–90
The five main areas of Flanders, each with its own brief introduction and an alphabetical listing of the main attractions.
    Practical information
    Snippets of 'Did you know...' information
    2 city walks
    3 drives
    Tips for those seeking peace and quiet

Where To... pages 91–116
Detailed listings of the best places to eat, stay, shop, take the children and be entertained.

Practical Matters pages 117–24
A highly visual section containing essential travel information.

Maps
All map references are to the individual maps found in the What to See section of this guide.
For example, Antwerp Zoo has the reference ✚ 34C4 – indicating the page on which the map is located and the grid square in which Antwerp Zoo is to be found.
A list of the maps that have been used in this travel guide can be found in the index.

Prices
Where appropriate, an indication of the cost of an establishment is given by **£** signs:
£££ denotes higher prices, **££** denotes average prices, while **£** denotes lower charges.

Star Ratings
Most of the places described in this book have been given a separate rating:

✪✪✪   Do not miss
✪✪   Highly recommended
✪   Worth seeing

Viewing
Flanders

Above: *the Cogels Osylei in the Antwerp
district of Zurenborg*
Right: *comic strip gable in Brussels*

A Personal View

Begijnhof
The *begijnhof*, or *béguinage*, is a community of lay sisters – a cross between a convent and an almshouse complex – living together within a town. The history of the begijnhofs goes back to the 12th century and they were especially prevalent in Belgium, Germany and The Netherlands.

Begijnhof in Bruges

Flanders is the Dutch-speaking half of Belgium. The region has its own parliament, its own language, flag and national anthem, and especially its own history. It is a history that is clearly present today.

Many market squares still retain something of the atmosphere of the Middle Ages, churches and museums are a testimony of the glory of the Golden Age, and proud belfries are a reminder of the power of the guilds.

The feeling that the Middle Ages are not so very long ago is reinforced by the many legends and figures from folklore that live on in daily life. The Flemish still cherish their heroes, colourful characters from the medieval adventurer-cum-prankster Till Eulenspiegel and his side-kick Lange Wapper to Reynard the Fox. Many of their traditions are based on these legendary characters. The inhabitants of Dendermonde still carry a model of the horse, Beiaard, through the streets. The residents of Ypres still throw cats (soft toys these days) from the top of the belfry to challenge the devil, and the two chopped-off hands in Antwerp's coat of arms directly refer to the legend about the origins of the city's name: *handwerpen* (throwing hands).

However rich the past may be, it can also be a hindrance at times. Flemish identity is as elusive today as historic Flanders was self-aware. The region seems to hesitate between chaos and order, between the centre of Europe and the provinces, between small-minded and Burgundian, and between *waterzooi* and *bisque de homard* – even the menu sits between extremes. Politically, too, the puzzle which is Flanders is still incomplete. This fact makes Flanders one of the most fascinating areas in Europe.

BEGIJNHOF

Flanders's Features

The People

Belgium covers a surface area of 30,500sq km and has just over ten million inhabitants. Approximately 60 percent of the population, some 5.9 million people, live in Flanders. The number of inhabitants of the metropolitan district of Brussels comes to almost 950,000. With a population density of 325 inhabitants per square kilometre, Belgium is one of the most densely populated countries in Europe.

Hospitable Flanders

The Flemish combine an easy-going attitude with a Burgundian lifestyle. Food and drink play an important part in daily life. Even the writer Victor Hugo, who thought that beer leaves 'the taste of dead mice' in the mouth, lived in Flanders for a long time.

Diamonds

The diamond trade makes a significant contribution to the Belgian economy. The import and export of diamonds total almost 23 billion dollars per year. The diamond trade is largely concentrated in Antwerp. This Scheldt city accounts for no less than 60 percent of the international diamond trade.

Port

The port of Antwerp also provides an important economic stimulus. The port, which tranships more than ten million tons of goods per year, is the second largest in Europe. The docks, terminals and container grounds stretch across an area of 14,000ha, while the port of Antwerp provides work for almost 60,000 people.

Quality chocolate shop in Bruges

Beer

On average, Belgians drink 118 litres of beer per year, giving them sixth ranking amongst other European nations. The 110 Belgian breweries account for an annual production of some 14.1 million hectolitres of beer. Nearly five million hectolitres of this is intended for export, which is still showing an upward trend. Speciality beers, in particular, such as white beer, beers brewed by trappist monasteries, and spontaneous-fermentation beers are increasingly popular abroad. But the best known are still the more conventional pilsener-type beers such as Stella Artois.

A Country Rich in Cafés

With one café to every 338 inhabitants, Flanders may call itself one of the most café-rich countries in the world. There are no less than 17,480 cafés, beer cellars, sailors' pubs, taverns and inns in Flanders. Going to the pub is a popular pastime here.

Essence of Flanders

Boat gable of De Vijf Werelddelen *(Antwerp)*

Gothic churches, buildings in art nouveau style, an enormous wealth of paintings, and an abundance of cafés and restaurants: a journey through Flanders is like immersing yourself in a warm bath. Busy cities such as Brussels, Antwerp and Ghent alternate with empty polders showing the odd church tower on the horizon. Begijnhofs (► 6) and abbeys lie hidden between large stretches of moorland, and in cities such as Bruges, Leuven and Dendermonde, the past lives on as if time has stood still for centuries. 'Flat Flanders' even has some mountains: in the south, small rivers wind their way down from the picturesque hilly landscape of Heuvelland, about which Rubens once said that he had 'never seen more delightful country'.

Hilly landscape in West Flanders

THE **10** ESSENTIALS

If you only have a short time to visit Flanders, or would like to attempt a complete picture of the country, here are the essentials:

• **Take a boat trip through Ghent or Bruges**, preferably in Spring, when the first visitors sit out on the terraces and the trees are heavy with blossom.

• **Order a cone of golden Flemish fries at the** *frietkot* **(chippy)** topped with a generous dollop of mayonnaise.

• **Go and see the paintings of van Dyck, Jordaens or Rubens** in one of the many churches and museums, such as the Antwerp St Jacobskerk or the Museum voor Schone Kunsten (▶ 32).

• **Listen to the sounds of the carillon** on a sultry summer's evening, in front of the St Romboutstoren in Mechelen.

• **Visit the begijnhof** (▶ 6) of Diest or Leuven and lose track of time while you meander.

• **Look at Manneken Pis in Brussels**, laugh at the reactions of other tourists,

and take a photograph just as the waterjet suddenly 'spouts out' (▶ 75).

• **Drink a** *pintje* **or** *Bolleke* at a terrace or at a *bruin café* (traditional pub), and watch the world go by.

• **Visit a Gothic cathedral or church** and light a candle for someone dear to you.

• **Admire jugglers, street artists and musicians** during the Gentse Feesten (Ghent town festival), in the third week of July (▶ 115).

• **Brush past the statue of Everard 't Serclaes** in the Grand-Place in Brussels. Touching the copper is said to bring luck (▶ 17).

Left: Jan Zonder Vrees, *one of the many pubs in Flanders*

Below: *the atmospheric Conscienceplein in Antwerp – an oasis of peace in the city centre*

The Shaping of Flanders

500 BC
Celtic tribes settle in what is now Belgium. The Nervii settle along the River Scheldt, and the Eburones build settlements along the River Meuse.

57 BC
Julius Caesar battles with the Celtic Belgae. It takes him five years to subdue the local tribes. The Emperor is said to have commented: 'Of all the Gallic peoples, the Belgians are the bravest'.

7th century
Large parts of Belgium are converted to Christianity. The current linguistic division comes into existence during this period: the language of communication in the north was Germanic, that of the south was Romanic.

King Albert monument in Nieuwpoort

Right: the elaborate gable of the Onze-Lieve-Vrouwe-kathedraal in Antwerp

862
Baudouin with the Iron Arm becomes the first Count of Flanders. The power of the principality increases during the following century. The influence and territory of the Duchy of Brabant also increase.

11 July 1302
Battle of the Golden Spurs. Belgian troops, mainly infantry, defeat the much better armed cavalry of the French, near Kortrijk (Courtrai). The riders' golden spurs are taken home as trophies.

1477
Charles the Bold is killed during the Occupation of Nancy. His daughter, Mary of Burgundy,

marries Maximilian of Austria, which places the Low Countries, by now one area, under Habsburg rule.

1500
Charles V, later Emperor Charles, is born in Ghent. During his reign, he manages to expand his territory to 'an empire where the sun never sets'.

1517
Martin Luther proclaims his new doctrine. Emperor Charles

attempts to halt the distribution of documents and ideas, and in doing so instigates the Inquisition. His son, Philip II, continues the fanatical persecution of all dissidents.

1568
Counts Egmont and Hoorn are decapitated in the Grand-Place in Brussels by order of the Spanish. This event signifies the start of the Eighty Years War. William of Orange leads the fight against Spanish occupation from the northern part of the Low Countries.

1585
The Catholic provinces which remain loyal to Spain unite in the Union of Atrecht. The Protestant provinces sign the Union of Utrecht. From this moment, the separation of the southern and northern parts of the Low Countries is a reality.

1714–95
Flanders is under Austrian rule. The country rises up during the Brabançon Revolt (1789), but the revolt is crushed by the Austrians. In 1795 the country passes into French hands.

1815
Battle of Waterloo. The armies of Prussia, England and The Netherlands bring Napoleon to a crushing defeat. Belgium and The Netherlands form the United Kingdom of The Netherlands, but internal differences soon lead to a break-up.

1831
Belgium becomes an independent state. Leopold of Saxe-Coburg-Gotha is crowned the first king.

1914–18
On 4 August, Germany invades Belgium. The Belgian army, led by King Albert I, retreats behind the IJzer. During the trench warfare which follows, mustard gas is used for the first time.

1930
The University of Ghent becomes Dutch-speaking.

1940
After an 18-day battle, the Belgian army is defeated by a German invasion force. Leopold III signs a weapons agreement, without consulting his government. He steps down in 1950 to make way for his son Baudouin.

1959
Brussels becomes the seat of the EEC.

1993
King Baudouin I dies. His brother Albert II succeeds him.

1994
Belgium becomes a federal state with directly elected community and district councils.

Tombs of Mary of Burgundy and Charles the Bold, Onze-Lieve-Vrouwekerk, Bruges

1

Peace & Quiet

The Eddy Merckx cycle route: in the tracks of 'The Cannibal'

Farmsteads and Abbeys

Although Flanders is one of the most densely populated regions in Europe, the countryside offers plenty of

opportunities to those who seek peace and quiet. The Kempen, the largest area of woodland in Flanders, stretches across the two northern provinces, Limburg and Antwerp. The landscape is characterised by extensive areas of moorland, alternating with pine forests, fens and sand drifts. The region is rich in farmsteads, abbeys and begijnhofs (▶ 6) , and is excellent walking and cycling country. With some 1,600km of cycle routes (46 signposted sections) and 300 touristic footpaths, there is plenty of choice.

Cycling Country
More and more holiday-makers are discovering that Flanders is ideal for cycling. The flat and gently rolling countryside is in many places ideal for making cycle trips, even if the wind in the polders can be troublesome. The number of cycle routes has increased considerably over the past decade. The routes often have a theme, such as the castle, abbey or smugglers' routes. Information on long-distance cycle routes is available from Recreatief fietsen ✉ Van Stralenstraat 40, Antwerp ☎ 03–2327218

Nature Reserves
A number of well-known areas and nature reserves, such as Het Zwin (▶ 26), the Flemish Ardennes (▶ 25) and the Haspengouw (▶ 18), are discussed elsewhere in this guide.

The Hills of Heuvelland

Anyone who thought that Flanders consists of no more than flat polders is in for a surprise. There are a number of treacherous humps in the southern landscape, such as the Kemmelberg (159m) in Heuvelland. This municipality consisting of eight villages is situated in an undulating landscape which stretches as far as the French border. Fields and pastures form a quilt of fast changing colours. When Rubens travelled through the area, he claimed that he had 'never seen more delightful country'.

The Sahara

Lovers of dunes and sea will be inclined to travel to the Flemish coast, but a warning is in order. Grim apartment blocks and concrete high-rise buildings dominate the skyline in many places. Fortunately, there are plenty of exceptions, such as the dunes at Wenduine and the Hoge Blekker near Koksijde (▶ 53), the highest dunes in Flanders. The beach at De Panne (▶ 56), just above the French border is, at least at low tide, one of the widest in Belgium, and a little further inland changes into an area of dunes with the rather dramatic name 'the Sahara'. Several film directors have shot desert scenes here.

River Country

Flanders is a country of rivers. There are several watery areas, such as the Leiestreek south of Ghent, the Meetjesland in the northeast of East Flanders, and the Maasland of Limburg. In this area around Kinrooi and Maasmechelen, water-sports enthusiasts will always find plenty to do. In between the windmills and reeds are a number of gravel quarries, which in the course of time have filled up with water. The valley landscape alternates with stretches of moorland, pine and deciduous forests. The extensive moorland near Maasmechelen is probably the best known.

Those who seek even more peace and quiet will find it in the wide IJzervlakte between the municipalities of Alveringem, Vleteren and Lo-Reninge: a green triangular area, which is especially breathtaking at sunrise and sunset.

The Zoniënwoud south of Brussels

Flanders's Famous

In this self-portrait, James Ensor parodied Rubens's famous Self-portrait with Hat

Charles V (1500–58)

Charles V (1500–58), or simply Emperor Charles, was born in Ghent in 1500. During his reign he expanded his territory to 'an empire where the sun never sets'. Charles endeavoured to create a United Kingdom of the Netherlands, but also gave the starting signal for the Inquisition.

Painters

In the Golden Age, Pieter Paul Rubens (1577–1640), Antoon (Anthony) van Dyck (1599–1641) and Jacob Jordaens (1593–1678) were leading painters with world-wide reputations. Their biblical representations and portraits of famous contemporaries can still be found in a large number of museums.

Pieter Bruegel the Elder (1525–69) is known for his allegorical representations, such as the *Dulle Griet*, with which he exposed the horrors of war. He was also fond of painting country fairs, for which he disguised himself as a farmer so as not to be recognised.

For a large part of his life, the Anglo-Belgian painter James Ensor (1860–1949) searched for the right technique to represent light in his paintings. Ensor was reviled by the leading art salons and, partly out of revenge, he caricatured the faces of prominent citizens into distorted masks.

Georges Rémi

Georges Rémi (1907–83) is better known under the pseudonym of Hergé, the name found on all the Tintin comic strip books. Rémi developed the comic book into fully-fledged story-telling. More than 200 million copies of Tintin's adventures have been sold world-wide. The success of Willy Vandersteen (1913–90), the spiritual father of Suske and Wiske, has also reached far beyond the national borders. The character of the vain but brave Lambik was based on the Antwerp model.

Jacques Brel

Jacques Brel (1929–78) was the grand master of the French *chanson*. Brel sang with an unrivalled passion about great love affairs, the flat countryside of Flanders, and about Brussels. He also acted in several films.

Eddy Merckx

The most famous Belgian sportsman is undoubtedly the racing cyclist Eddy Merckx (1945–). Merckx won the Tour de France and the Tour of Italy five times, and triumphed in so many classic races that other cyclists gave him the nickname 'The Cannibal'.

Top Ten

Above: *gables in the
Grand-Place in Brussels*
Right: *spire of the
Brussels Town Hall*

1
Dodengang and IJzertoren, Diksmuide

Dodengang

✉ IJzerdijk 65

☎ 051–505534

🕐 Apr–Sep: daily 10–12 and 1–5

✋ Free

IJzertoren

✉ IJzerdijk 49

☎ 051–500286

🕐 Easter holiday–11 Nov: Mon–Sun 9–12 and 1–5; Jun–Aug: 9–12 and 1–6; Jul–Aug: also open Sat–Sun lunchtime from 10

♿ Good

✋ Moderate

↔ Veurne (► 56)

The Dodengang, one of the most dangerous sets of trenches during World War I

The Dodengang and IJzertoren are silent but impressive testimonies of the destruction of World War I.

Just outside the small town of Diksmuide (► 49) are the preserved remains of one of the most dangerous sets of Belgian trenches: the **Dodengang** (Trench of Death). During World War I this was an advanced post of the Belgian lines, at a distance of barely 50m from a German bunker. In order to reach the lines at the back, the Flemish soldiers had to cross two footbridges within firing range of the Germans. Many lost their lives.

Further on at the IJzerdijk stands the **IJzertoren**, a memorial to the Flemish soldiers who died at the front in World War I. The tower is also a symbol of Flemish resistance.

During the war, some 80 percent of the Belgian army came from Flanders. The army leadership, however, was mainly French-speaking. Some Dutch-speaking soldiers were unable to understand the orders given by their superiors and were needlessly sent to their deaths. The soldiers are still honoured with the letters AVV–VVK, standing for *Alles voor Vlaanderen – Vlaanderen voor Kirstos* (All for Flanders – Flanders for Christ).

The IJzertoren is a politically charged monument. In 1946 the tower was blown up with dynamite by unknown persons. A new monument, the Paxpoort, then rose from its ashes. The new 84m IJzertoren was rebuilt in 1951 and is the largest war memorial in Europe. The annual pilgrimage to the tower, where there is also a museum, draws people from around the world. Unfortunately, it is also frequented by some groups with extreme right-wing and nationalist tendencies.

The IJzertoren also contains the chapel of Onze-Lieve-Vrouw van de IJzer. The original design of the stained glass windows is based on drawings by Joe English, a soldier at the front who lost his life here. On the first floor is a small war museum.

2

Grand-Place (Grote Markt), Brussels

The Grand-Place in Brussels is considered to be one of the most beautiful squares in the world and is an oasis of light and peace in the heart of the city.

The Grand-Place (Grote Markt) in Brussels is a square that is unrivalled in Belgium. The many statues, reliefs and balustrades in baroque style are ravishing. Jean Cocteau called it 'the most beautiful theatre in the world'.

The market square would have looked considerably less impressive had the French King Louis XIV not subjected the city to heavy artillery during the 15th century. The firing reduced most of the square to ashes, but the inhabitants of Brussels managed to rebuild it within four years.

The Grand-Place is dominated by the 15th-century **Hôtel de Ville** or **Stadhuis** (Town Hall) an elegant building in pure Gothic style, whose 97m tower rises high above the city centre. The Maison du Roi opposite served, amongst other things, as the residence of the Dukes of Brabant and as a prison. The original wooden building on the site was a bread market, hence it was known as the 'bread house'. Nowadays, you will find Manneken Pis's wardrobe in this house.

The gables of the guild houses clearly show the struggle for prestige among the guilds. When the sun catches the gold leaf on the gables, the square shines in all its glory.

Close to the Town Hall is the memorial statue to Everard 't Serclaes, a resistance fighter who, as head of one hundred rebels, chased the Flemish garrison out of town.

The copper of the statue shines as if it has just been polished. This is because most passers-by like to brush past the statue. The residents of Brussels are convinced that this brings luck.

74B3

Hôtel de Ville (Stadhuis)

Grand-Place (Grote Markt)

02–2794365

Guided tours in English: Apr–Sep: Tue 11:30, 3:15, Wed 3:15, Sun 12:15, Oct–Mar: Tue 11:30, 3:15, Wed 3:15. Guided tours in Dutch: Apr–Sep: Tue–Wed 1:45, Sun 11:30; Oct–Mar: Tue–Wed 1:45. Closed on 1 Jan, 1 May, 1 Nov, 11 Nov and 25 Dec

Various café-restaurants in the Grand-Place, such as La Maison du Cygne (£££) and Roy D'Espagne (£)

Beurs

Good

Cheap

Manneken Pis (▶ 75), St Hubert Galleries (▶ 77)

Every other year, the Grand-Place in Brussels is covered with an enormous carpet of flowers

3

Haspengouw

The Haspengouw is known as the orchard of Belgium. Especially in spring, when the fruit trees blossom, the landscape is breathtakingly beautiful.

Kasteel van Rijkel near Borgloon

 31E1

Alden Biesen

✉ Kasteelstraat 6, Bilzen

☎ 089–519344

🕐 Free entrance to classic gardens. Castle open during exhibitions: Mon–Fri 9–12 and 1–5, Sat–Sun 10–12 and 1–4

♿ Good

✋ Free, except during exhibitions

Bezoekerscentrum Alden Biesen (educative nature museum)

🕐 Apr–Sep: Mon–Sun 10–6

✋ Moderate

Kasteel van Rijkel

✉ Van Leeuwenstraat 23, Borgloon

☎ 011–691188

🕐 The castle can be partly viewed Mon–Fri 9–12; Apr–Sep: also Sat–Sun 10–6

🍴 Brasserie (££), Grote Markt Tongeren; Kanunnikenhof (£££), Vermeulenstraat, Tongeren

↔ Tongeren (➤ 89), St Truiden (➤ 88)

No other area is as abundant in fruit as the Haspengouw, a beautiful undulating region in the southeast of Flanders. The apple, pear and cherry orchards alternate with extensive fields and sunken roads, which are typical of this region.

Although the countryside looks completely different each season, the best time to visit the Haspengouw is spring, when the fruit trees are in blossom and a haze of white, pink and red envelops the landscape.

The Haspengouw is a rural area. The villages are generally small and often consist of no more than a circle of houses around a church or castle. It is no surprise, therefore, that Belgium's smallest village, Herstappe, is found here. It has a surface area of 135ha and 85 inhabitants.

In addition to the numerous orchards, the Haspengouw is also known for its many square farmsteads and castles, which are spread across the countryside. The 13th-century estate of **Alden Biesen** is considered to be the largest castle complex in Belgium. There are also interesting castles around the medieval village of Borgloon, currently the heart of the fruit region, such as **Kasteel van Rijkel**, a moated U-shaped castle in Maasland style, now the home of the Haspengouw Tourist Board.

Its fertile soil also makes the Haspengouw an attractive area from a culinary point of view. It is known for a number of gastronomic favourites, such as Borgloon wine, fruit flan (*vlaai*) and plum gin. The mushrooms cultivated in the marl caves according to traditional methods are definitely worth a try.

Orchard in the Haspengouw

4
Leiestreek

Museum van Deinze en de Leiestreek

✉ Lucien Matthijslaan 3–5, Deinze

☎ 09-3819670

🕐 Tue–Fri 2–5:30, Sat–Sun 10–12 and 2–5 closed on 1 Jan and 25 Dec

♿ Good

✋ Cheap

Museum Dhondt-Dhaenens

✉ Museumlaan 14, Deurle

☎ 09-2835123

🕐 Wed–Fri 2–6, Sat–Sun 10–12 and 2–6 (in winter until 5). Closed on 21 Dec and 8 Feb

♿ Good

✋ Cheap

Castle of Ooidonk

✉ Ooidonkdreef, Deinze

☎ 09-2826123/ 09-3819501

🕐 Easter–15 Sep: Sun and national holidays 2–5; Jul–Aug: also Sat

✋ Moderate

At the beginning of the 20th century, The Leie district was an important source of inspiration for painters and sculptors. The region is still considered to be very idyllic.

Southwest of Ghent (► 60), the wide River Leie winds its way through a gentle landscape. The area became well known partly because of groups of painters and sculptors who regularly came here and were inspired by the unspoiled landscape.

The group, which became known as the Latem School, was an important influence on Flemish 20th-century painting. Artists such as van den Woestyne, van den Abeele, Permeke and Servaes are still known beyond Flanders. Much of their work can be seen at the **Museum van Deinze en de Leiestreek** and the **Museum Dhondt-Dhaenens** in Deurle.

To supplement their income, some artists were supported by rich benefactors from Ghent. In the woods around the area you can still catch a glimpse of the country houses of some of these patrons.

The Leiestreek is a green part of Flanders. It is an area rich in water and therefore not only a paradise for pleasure boats, but also excellent cycling and walking country. There are a number of long-distance footpaths along the Leie river, such as the GR128 between Ghent and Deinze.

The indisputable showpiece of the region is **Castle of Ooidonk**. This castle was built in the 16th century with a mixture of Flemish and Spanish architecture, but after subsequent renovations acquired the appearance of a Renaissance castle which would not have looked out of place along the French Loire. In one of the rooms hangs a portrait of one of its former owners: Philip of Montmorency, better known as Count van Hoorn.

The winding River Leie is ideal for taking boat-trips

5
Ostend

In the 19th century, Ostend was a popular resort among the beau monde. One or two places still exude some of the period atmosphere.

At the sight of the high-rise buildings which now spoil the view of the Ostend coast, you may well wonder how this town could ever have been called 'Queen of the Seaside Resorts'. In the 19th century, however, Ostend was *the* haunt of the aristocracy. Rich ladies would come to breathe the gentle sea air, and gentlemen tried their luck at the races or in the casino.

Leopold II, too, had a weak spot for Ostend. The king often stayed at a villa by the beach with two arcades. Behind these arcades, the prestigious Thermae Palace Hotel was later built, a sophisticated luxury hotel with a health centre for the Belgian beau monde. Although the villa is no longer frequented by royalty and health-centre fanatics have long since departed for more exotic climes, you can still sense the 19th-century atmosphere here.

This also applies to the Wellington Racecourse at the back, an antique hippodrome where, during race meetings, the stands are still peopled by gamblers and bookmakers (▶ 114).

At the start of the Groot Strand (large beach) stands the monumental **Casino Kuursaal**. The gambling halls with roulette and baccarat tables are a sight in themselves. One of the halls is decorated with frescos by Paul Delvaux.

Ostend is also the city of James Ensor. This Anglo-Belgian painter, famous for his carnival masks and distorted faces, lived and worked here for a considerable time. The **Ensorhuis**, his former house, has been restored to resemble a colourful and very atmospheric junk shop. His original salon-workshop displays many objects from his studio. There are several original Ensor paintings at the **Museum voor Schone Kunsten**.

Thermae Palace Hotel: no longer a spa, but now a prestigious hotel

 30A3

Casino Kuursaal

 Monacoplein

☎ 059–705111

🕓 Gambling room Tue–Sun from 3PM

Ensorhuis

✉ Vlaanderenstraat 27

☎ 059–805335

🕓 Mon–Sun 10–12 and 2–5. Closed on 1 Jan and 25 Dec

💵 Cheap

Museum voor Schone Kunsten

✉ Wapenplein

☎ 059–805335

🕓 See Ensorhuis. Closed on 1 Jan, 15 May, 18 Sep and 25 Dec

🍴 Se@Site (£), Alfons Pieterslaan; De Mosselbeurs (££), Dwarsstraat; Villa Maritza (£££), Albert I–Promenade

 Moderate

6
Rubenshuis, Antwerp

✚ 31D3

✉ Wapper

☎ 03-2324747

🕓 Tue–Sun 10–5. Closed
on 1–2 Jan,
1 May, Ascension,
1–2 Nov and 25–26 Dec

🍴 Rubens Inn (£), Wapper

🚌 Meir 2, 3, 15

✋ Cheap

↔ St Jacobskerk (▶ 35)

The Rubens House is one of Antwerp's most interesting attractions. A guided tour through the house is a voyage of discovery in the footsteps of the baroque painter.

A visit to Antwerp would not be complete without a visit to the Rubenshuis. This former residence and workshop of Antwerp's greatest painter not only contains a number of magnificent paintings, but also conveys an impression of the lifestyle of Antwerp's wealthier citizens.

Rubens bought the house in the Wapper in 1610 and had it converted to a Renaissance residence of Italian appeal. The baroque portico between the courtyard and the garden was designed by the painter himself.

A visit to the house leads past a production workshop, an antechamber with gold leather furnishings, and the workshop where life models posed in private.

The Rubenshuis contains a number of the master's canvases, including *The Annunciation*, in which the Archangel Gabriel tells Mary that she will be the mother of Christ. In the dining room hangs a famous self-portrait. Some say that the hat worn by the elderly Rubens in this painting was a way of hiding the fact that he was beginning to go bald. There are also several paintings by other artists.

The art room which Rubens, just like his contemporaries, furnished to impress his visitors, is also noteworthy. The painter received very prominent guests here, including the Archduke Albert and Archduchess Isabella. Due to his contacts in higher places, Rubens not only became a painter who was much in demand, but also ensured that he was frequently asked to participate in secret diplomatic missions.

Interior of the Rubenshuis; in the background is a famous self-portrait

7

St Baafskathedraal, Ghent

St Baafskathedraal is especially famous for its large number of art treasures, including the superb The Adoration of the Mystic Lamb.

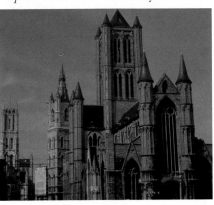

St Baafskathedraal in Ghent

One of the most striking buildings in the centre of Ghent is St Baafskathedraal. This cathedral, and the interior in particular, is a veritable treasure trove. The most remarkable treasures include an oak and marble pulpit by the 18th-century sculptor Laurent Delvaux and the painting *The Vocation of St Bavo* by Rubens (1623).

In a separate area, **The Adoration of the Mystic Lamb** (1432) is exhibited behind bulletproof glass. Many believe that this is the most beautiful Flemish painting ever made. The 'mystic lamb' represents the mystery of the Redemption. By sacrificing the lamb, mankind can atone for original sin. *The Adoration of the Mystic Lamb* is a triptych, with each panel telling a story. The painting is especially famous for its superb detail. If you look carefully, you can see the towers of Utrecht and Bruges cathedrals in the city in the background of the main panel. Note also the folds in the red cloak of the sitting figure, in the middle of the painting, who represents God. In total, no less than 248 figures are portrayed.

The Adoration of the Mystic Lamb is officially attributed to the two van Eyck brothers. Curiously enough, other works are known by only one of the two brothers, Jan van Eyck. The second brother, Hubert van Eyck, is supposed to have died as early as 1426, which makes his contribution to *The Adoration of the Mystic Lamb* extremely dubious, and the mystery surrounding the canvas even more intriguing.

✚ 30C2

✉ St Baafsplein

☎ 09-2251626

🕐 Apr–Oct: Mon–Sun 8:30–6; Nov–Mar: Mon–Sun 8:30–5

🍴 Faits Divers (££), Korenmarkt

🚌 Korenmarkt bus/tram 1, 10, 11, 12, 13

✋ Free

The Adoration of the Mystic Lamb

🕐 Apr–Oct: Mon–Sat 9:30–5, Sun 1–5; Nov–Mar: Mon–Sat 10:30–12 and 2:30–4, Sun 2–5

✋ Moderate

⬌ Belfort (► 60)

❓ With the ticket needed to view *The Adoration of the Mystic Lamb*, you can also visit the 12th-century crypt, under the choir.

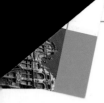

8
Stadhuis, Leuven

✝ 31D2

✉ Grote Markt 9

☎ 016–211540

🕐 Salons and council
chamber open to
visitors. The other
rooms may be viewed
during a guided tour:
Apr– Sep: Mon–Fri 11,
3, Sat–Sun 3; Oct–Mar:
Mon–Sun 3. Closed on
1 Jan and 25 Dec

🍴 Gambrinus (£)

🚌 Fochplein

✋ Cheap

↔ Fonske (► 79)

*The gable of Leuven
Town Hall barely contains
a flat surface*

*Leuven Town Hall looks like a giant Gothic
shrine. Its gable is so ornate that there is
barely a flat surface in sight.*

As you walk across the Grote Markt in Leuven (Louvain),
the exuberant 15th-century Town Hall is immediately
arresting. When the building of the Town Hall started, the
city wanted to surpass that of its neighbour, Brussels.
Since it was impossible for the Leuven building to
distinguish itself upwards (a clock tower was not viable, as
the ground was too soft), the builders tried to make
an impact through architectural and sculptural decorations.
This approach can certainly be called successful. The
many parapets, pinnacles, dormer windows and small
niches ensure that the building looks like an enormous
religious shrine.

The lower parts of the niches portray scenes from the
Bible on the theme of sin and punishment. These
representations served not only to educate people, but
also as a warning to the judges who sat in the building at
that time.

The alcoves themselves were empty, until the writer
Victor Hugo had the idea of
filling them with statues. The
ground floor shows artists,
scholars and other prominent
people from the history of
Leuven. On the first floor are the
patron saints of the parishes,
followed by the Counts of
Leuven and the Dukes of
Brabant on the second floor.

The hall of the Town Hall,
open to the public, includes a
statue of Fiere Margriet (Proud
Margaret), the patron saint of
servant girls: St Margaret of
Leuven. After her employers
were murdered in front of her,
one of the murderers asked her
to marry him. When she
refused, Fiere Margriet was
raped and murdered, after
which her body was carried
miraculously into the city on the
River Dijle. Her grave can be
found in the eighth chapel of the
St Pieterskerk opposite.

9

The Flemish Ardennes

*The Flemish Ardennes are far less well-known
and are not as high as their Walloon counterparts.
Nevertheless, this area in the south of Flanders
has much to offer the holidaymaker.*

View of Ronse

The Flemish Ardennes form a varied area with wooded slopes, green hilltops and romantic old water-mills.

In contrast with the Walloon Ardennes, which are often steeper, the Flemish Ardennes consist mainly of an undulating and pleasant countryside. Nevertheless, cyclists do sometimes have to make considerable efforts to stay in the saddle.

There are some atmospheric towns in this region, such as the artists' village Kwaremont with its many workshops, and Oudenaarde, which after Ghent is the most important art city in East Flanders. The Zwalmstreek, with its 12 easy-going villages in the valley surrounding the River Zwalm is attractive country for walking (► 67).

For many people the small town of Ronse (Renaix) is the jewel in the Flemish Ardennes. Ronse owes this honorary title especially to its location, although few tourists would be attracted by the town in itself. The most important sight in Ronse is the **St Hermescrypte**, the beautiful Romanesque crypt of St Hermeskerk, where the relics of St Hermes are kept. During the Middle Ages, the crypt was a place of pilgrimage for the mentally ill, who sprinkled themselves with water from the well, in the hope that they would emerge as 'normal'. A mural behind the church shows that St Hermes must have been a much-visited saint.

Near Ronse is the highest point of the Flemish Ardennes, the 141m-high Kluisberg. The most beautiful time to visit the area is April or May, when blue hyacinths are flowering on the slopes.

✚ 30B1

St Hermescrypte

✉ Kaatsspelplein, Ronse

☎ 055–232812

🕐 Easter–Sep: Tue–Fri 10–12 and 1:30–5, Sat–Sun 10–12 and 2:30–5:30

🍴 The Look (££), Priestersstraat, Ronse

♿ Few

💰 Cheap

↔ Geraardsbergen (► 65), Oudenaarde (► 66)

10
Het Zwin

This nature reserve and bird sanctuary is an area rich in water and is a haven for walkers and bird-watchers. In the summer, the sea lavender lends the area a purple hue.

Het Zwin nature reserve

Situated north of Knokke (► 53), just below the Dutch border, lies one of the most unusual nature reserves in Flanders. Het Zwin is partly linked to the North Sea. During spring or storm tides, large parts of the area are flooded. The presence of the salty seawater has enabled a number of unique plant species to develop, such as sea lavender. In addition, many minuscule water plants and molluscs find a home here.

For migrating and winter birds, such as sandpipers and black-bellied plovers, Het Zwin is an ideal spot to spend the winter. The many bird species which nest here every year also include a group of storks. If you are lucky, you will see them flapping their wings high up on their nests.

In the Middle Ages, Het Zwin was the most important estuary in Europe. The water served as an open link with Bruges and Damme, until the area slowly silted up with sand. At the initiative of Count Léon Lippens, it was declared a designated nature reserve in 1952.

These days, Het Zwin is the most important area of mud flats and salt marshes in Belgium. Mud flats are overgrown sandbars, which are flooded twice a day while salt marshes flood only at spring tide, so that small plants such as samphire can grow here. The best time to visit Het Zwin is in the summer, when the area glows with an enchanting purple hue as a result of the flowering sea lavender or *zwinneblomme*.

Unfortunately, this salt-loving plant is threatened with extinction. The *zwinneblomme* is sold in bouquets of dried flowers and attracts many professional plant thieves. In an attempt to protect this threatened plant from illegal pickers, the fields are patrolled by guards during the day in the flowering season.

✚ 30B3

✉ Graaf Léon Lippensdreef 8

☎ 050–607086

🕐 Easter–Sep: Mon–Sun 9–7; Oct–Easter 9–5; Nov–Mar: closed Wed

🍴 Ten Bos (££), Blickeartlaan, Knokke-Heist

✋ Moderate

↔ Vlindertuin (► 53)

What to See

Above: the River
Nete near Lier
Right: Lange
Wapper, the giant
who can shrink
to the size of
a mouse

Antwerp and Surroundings

A visit to the province of Antwerp will inevitably involve a visit to the city of the same name. Antwerp was the cultural centre of Europe as early as the 16th century. The Onze-Lieve-Vrouwekathedraal and the paintings of Rubens and van Dyck are still famous beyond the city's borders.

Antwerp's port is the economic artery of an extensive hinterland. The container terminals and docks, north of the city, stretch as far as the Dutch border. The rest of the province is largely taken up by the Kempen, the largest green area in Flanders. Between the extensive woodlands and moorlands lie many historically interesting towns, such as Mechelen, the former capital of the Burgundian Netherlands, and Lier, which deservedly is often called 'Little Bruges'.

> *'This city is delightful.*
> *Paintings in the churches,*
> *carvings on the houses,*
> *Rubens*
> *in the chapels. The place is*
> *teeming with art.'*

VICTOR HUGO

•

Left: *The Zimmertoren in Lier*

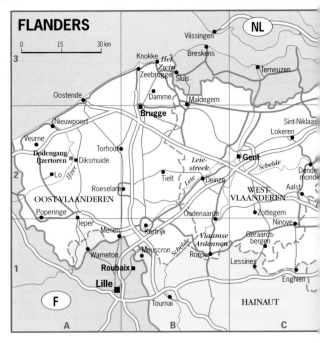

FLANDERS

Antwerp

When Napoleon visited Antwerp at the end of the 18th century, he imagined himself to be in 'an African village'. The writer Victor Hugo was considerably more positive: 'The place is teeming with art', he wrote.

Nowadays, a case can be made for both opinions. On the one hand, there is the thoughtlessly sited new architecture, which is an eyesore in the city centre, and on the other hand, there are the ornate guild houses, medieval alleyways and squares lined with numerous cafés, which lend Antwerp its charm.

Antwerp is an abundant city. This applies not only to the Scheldt and the beer which so freely flows from the taps of its pubs, but also to the rich cultural history – of which many buildings and art works are reminders, from the Rubenshuis to the Steen and from the Museum voor Schone Kunsten to the Stadhuis. Moreover, Antwerp is a wonderful city to stroll through. The centre is well organised and compact, so

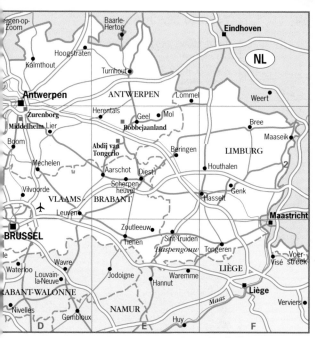

visitors can find it easily, whether or not they are guided by the spire of the Onze-Lieve-Vrouwekathedraal.

The chopped-off hand of the giant Antigoon in the Brabo Fountain

What to See in Antwerp

GROTE MARKT AND BRABO FOUNTAIN   ✪✪✪

🕇 34A3/4
✉ Grote Markt
🍴 Den Engel, Ultimatum (£)
🚇 Groenmarkt
🔁 Stadhuis (▶ 35)

The fine guild houses around the Grote Markt leave little doubt as to the source of Antwerp's wealth: trade and more trade. The Brabo Fountain in the square represents the legend from which Antwerp supposedly derives its name. A giant named Antigoon once tyrannised the Scheldt by demanding half the load from each passing skipper. If a skipper refused, his hand was chopped off. This continued until the Roman warrior Silvius Brabo eventually defeated the giant and threw his hand into the Scheldt. It is said that the term for hand-throwing (*handwerpen*) evolved into the Flemish name Antwerpen.

*Stadhuis with
Brabo Fountain*

OPENLUCKTMUSEUM MIDDELHEIM   ✪✪✪

🕇 31D2
✉ Middelheimlaan 61
☎ 03–8271534
🕐 Tue–Sun 10–5; Apr and Sep: until 7; May and Aug: until 8; Jun–Jul until 9. Closed 1–2 Jan, 1 May, Ascension Day, 1–2 Nov, 25–26 Dec
🎟 Free

In 1955, Antwerp was host to a large international open-air exhibition. The exhibition was such a success that the then burgomaster, Craeybeckx, decided to open a permanent museum on the same spot in Beeldenpark Middelheim. The sculptures and plastic models are situated in a park-like landscape and are spread over two pavilions. The collection includes such well-known names as Rodin, Zadkine and Henry Moore.

MUSEUM VOOR SCHONE KUNSTEN   ✪✪

🕇 34A1
✉ Leopold de Waelplaats
☎ 03–2387809
🕐 Daily 10–5. Closed 1–2 Jan, 1 May, Ascension Day, 25 Dec
♿ Good
🎟 Moderate

The Museum voor Schone Kunsten is located in South Antwerp, which the residents of the city call 'het Zuid'. This district, which also houses the Museum voor Fotografie (photography) and the Museum voor Hedendaagse Kunst (contemporary art), is also called Petit Paris, because of its wide avenues and distant vistas.

The collection includes work by Rubens, Ensor, Frans Hals, Modigliani and Titian.

ONZE-LIEVE-VROUWEKATHEDRAAL ✪✪

The 123m-high tower of the Onze-Lieve-Vrouwekathedraal rises high above the surrounding buildings. The cathedral was built between 1352 and 1521 in Gothic style. Initially, the intention was to give it five enormous towers.

Half-way through the building work, however, it transpired that this was not viable. Inside you will find a number of the greatest works of art in Flanders, such as Rubens' *Descent from the Cross* (1612).

But the cathedral came within a hair's breadth of being demolished. The city architect Blom, who had been commissioned by the French to carry out the demolition, turned out to be such a procrastinator that the operation was eventually called off by the French.

Descent from the Cross
by Rubens

🚩 34A3
✉ Handschoenmarkt
☎ 03–2139940
🕐 Mon–Fri 10–5, Sat 10–3, Sun and holidays 1–4. Closed 1 Jan
💷 Cheap

PUTKEVIE WELL ✪

'It's teeming with art here', exclaimed Victor Hugo when he visited Antwerp in the 19th century. To obtain a better view of a gable, he moved back a few steps and bumped into the well which still stands at the Handschoenmarkt, diagonally in front of the entrance to the Onze-Lieve-Vrouwekathedraal. The stone well with its iron canopy is by Quinten Metsys, who became a painter 'out of love'. Metsys was a blacksmith until he fell in love with the daughter of a painter. To increase his chances with her father, he acquired artistic skills and became one of the greatest painters of his time.

🚩 34A3
✉ Handschoenmarkt
🍴 Schaduw van de Kathedraal (£); Rooden Hoed (££)
🚌 Groenplaats

RUBENSHUIS (▶ 22, TOP TEN)

DID YOU KNOW?

According to the *Financial Times*, nowhere in the world are there as many quadrilingual people as in Flanders. You could even say that the Flemish know five languages, as many inhabitants of Antwerp consider their city dialect to be a language in itself.

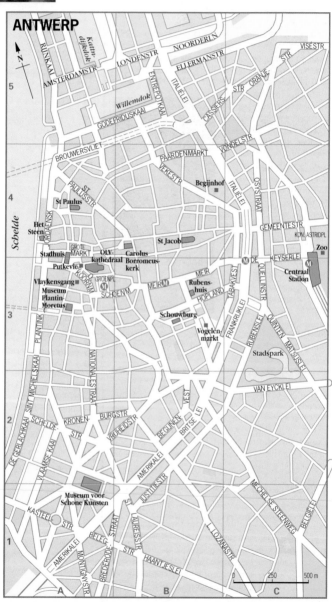

ANTWERP

Baroque gable of St Carolus Borromeuskerk

ST CAROLUS BORROMEUSKERK ✪✪

St Carolus Borromeus Church is situated in what is probably the most atmospheric square in Antwerp. This Italianate church, built by Jesuits between 1615 and 1621, came into existence during the aftermath of the Counter-Reformation. In this period, the Catholic Church tried to win back lapsed believers by means of pomp and circumstance. Rubens was partly responsible for the decoration of the gable.

➕ 34B4
✉ Hendrik Conscienceplein 12
☎ 03-2338433
🕐 Mon–Fri 10–12:30, 2–5, Sat 10–12:30, 2–7
♿ Reasonable
🎟 Free

ST JACOBSKERK ✪✪

East of the centre, the truncated tower of St Jacobs Church is one of the city's most recognisable and striking sights. The wide base is a result of an amended building plan. The well-to-do middle classes who lived in this district in Rubens' day, initially wanted a church which would surpass the Onze-Lieve-Vrouwekathedraal not only in splendour, but also in height. These ambitions were soon overtaken by reality. The art in the church includes work by Jordaens, van Dyck and de Vos. Behind the main altar is Rubens' grave. The master is buried beneath one of his own paintings, *Madonna and Child with Saints*.

➕ 34B4
✉ Lange Nieuwstraat 73
☎ 03-2321032
🕐 Apr–Oct: Mon–Fri 2–5
♿ Few
🎟 Cheap
🔁 Rubenshuis (➤ 22)

STADHUIS ✪✪

At the height of its wealth, Antwerp wanted to present itself as a modern and progressive city. The new Town Hall, built in 1565, was the most important showpiece for this. The architect, Cornelis Floris de Vriendt, was particularly inspired by Italian master-builders. The result, a mixture of Flemish–Italian Renaissance, has since become known as the Floris style. The eagle at the top of the building looks towards the emperor's city Aachen (Aix-la-Chapelle), which at that time was the seat of the Holy Roman Empire.

➕ 34A3
✉ Grote Markt
☎ 03-2211333
🕐 Guided tours: Mon–Fri 11, 2 and 3. Closed Thu
🎟 Cheap
🔁 Brabo Fountain (➤ 32)

THE STEEN ✪

🞣 34A4
✉ Steenplein 1
☎ 03–2320850
🕐 Tue–Sun 10–5. Closed
   1–2 Jan, 1 May,
   Ascension Day, 1–2
   Nov and 25–26 Dec
✋ Moderate

The Steen is on the site of the city's first settlement. Initially, the fort was the residence of the margrave but this somewhat grim building now houses the Scheepvaartmuseum (Maritime Museum). The crucifix opposite the entrance is a reminder of the time when the Steen was used as a prison. Those condemned to death muttered their last prayer here until 1823. Only the Steen fortress survived when the Scheldt quays were laid out in the 19th century.

VOGELENMARKT ✪

🞣 34B3
✉ Theaterplein
🕐 Sun 8–1PM
🍴 Various café–restaurants
   at the Graanmarkt and
   the Arme Duivelstraat
   (££–£)

The Vogelenmarkt is probably the best-known flea market in Belgium. This market, which takes place at the Theaterplein every Sunday, has grown into a top tourist attraction, especially popular with the Dutch. It derives its character not just from the table lamps, plastic knick-knacks and cheap lingerie on sale, but also from the atmosphere of the surrounding district, the Quartier Latin.

VLAYKENSGANG ✪✪

🞣 34A3
✉ Vlaykensgang
🍴 Sir Anthony van Dijck
   (£££)
🚇 Groenplaats
↔ Onze-Lieve-Vrouwe-
   kathedraal (▶ 32)

A stone's throw from the Handschoenmarkt is the Vlaykensgang, a medieval alleyway, where time seems to stand still. The name of the alleyway may be a reminder of the time when there was a *vlaaienhuis* (flan shop) here.

At the end of the alleyway is a restaurant named the Sir Anthony van Dijck. The chef and restaurant owner, Marc Paesbrugghe, is partly known for handing back his two Michelin stars (▶ 93). In the summer, residents of Antwerp go to the Vlanykensgang to listen to the carillon concerts from the nearby cathedral.

Above: *the Steen, seen from the Scheldt quayside*

ZOO ✪✪

Antwerp Zoo is one of the most famous zoos in the world. It was built in 1843 when it was considered fairly revolutionary to show animals in this way. In addition to giraffes, elephants and penguins, the zoo is home to some 5,000 other animals. It also has some fine examples of 19th-century architecture, such as the Egyptian elephant temple and the rhinoceros building. If you hear a station announcement in between the lions' roars, you are not mistaken. Centraal Station is immediately behind the imitation rocks at the back of the zoo.

🏛 34C4
✉ Koningin Astridplein 26
☎ 03–2024540
🕐 Opening hours vary according to the season: winter: 9–4:30, summer 9–6:15
♿ Good
💰 Expensive

ZURENBORG ✪✪✪

Near Berchem station is one of the most curious architectural creations in Flanders. The domain of Zurenborg was converted into a residential neighbourhood for the bourgeoisie at the end of the 19th century. The residents, all of whom were allowed to choose their own architect, tried their utmost to outdo each other.

The result is a colourful collection of mansions with art-nouveau and Jugendstil influences. The prestigious Cogels Osylei forms the district's central axis (► 5).

🏛 31D2
✉ Cogels Osylei, Guldenvliesstraat, Transvaalstraat, Pretoriastraat
🍴 Various café/restaurants in the Dageraadplaats, including De Verloren Onschuld (£) and De Schraele Troost (£)
🚌 Halte Tramplaats: bus 6, 34, tram 9, 11; halte Guldenvliesstraat: tram 8, 16
🚆 NMBS Berchem

Lioness at Antwerp Zoo

A City Walk Through Antwerp

Distance
4km (2.5 miles)

Time
3.5 hours (with a break)

Start point
Grote Markt
✚ 34A3/4

End point
Hendrik Conscienceplein
✚ 34B4

Lunch
Mamado (£)
✉ Conscienceplein 13
☎ 03–2319601

The Vleeshuis, former venue of the butchers' guild

From the Grote Markt, turn right into Suikerrui, cross the Jordaenskaai and go over the footbridge.

The walkway along the River Scheldt was built in 1885 and from here the inhabitants of Antwerp could watch at close quarters the loading and off-loading of large Congo boats.

Walk down and turn left onto the Steenplein.

This square is dominated by a medieval fort which looks fairly grim: the Steen (➤ 36). In front of the entrance is the statue of Lange Wapper, a giant who could shrink to the size of a mouse and would frighten drunkards on their way home.

Cross the quayside and take the Palingbrug. Pass by the striped building on the right and turn left into the Vleeshouwersstraat; take the third turning on your right, the Veemarkt.

At the Veemarkt stands the famous St Pauluskerk where you will find a number of beautiful paintings by Rubens.

Turn right in front of the church, into the Zirkstraat. Via the Lange Koepoortstraat (right turn), the Jeruzalemstraat (left turn) and the Coppenolstraat (left turn), you will reach the Minderbroedersstraat. At the end, turn right into the Blindestraat, which further on changes into the Prinsstraat. Take the second turning on the right, the Prinsesstraat, and go straight into St Jacobsstraat.

On the left-hand side you will find the church with the richest interior in Antwerp, the St Jacobskerk (➤ 35). The painter Rubens is buried here.

Turn right into the Lange Nieuwstraat; then take the third street on your right, the Katelijnevest. At the junction, go via the Wijngaardbrug into the Wolstraat. The Wijngaardstraat (left turn) will lead you to Hendrik Conscienceplein.

Here, in the most beautiful square in Antwerp, stands the St Carolus Borromeuskerk (➤ 35), a worthy point to conclude this walk.

Excursions from Antwerp and Surroundings

TONGERLO ABBEY ✪

An avenue of ancient lime trees leads to Tongerlo Abbey. The abbey was founded in 1130 by a small group of monks, who spent part of their time brewing beer and baking bread – items that can still be bought in the nearby shop. Close to the abbey is the Da Vinci Museum, whose collection consists of a single work of art. For those who have not had the opportunity to see the original in Milan, this oldest and best replica of *The Last Supper* by Leonardo da Vinci is worth seeing.

➕ Not on the map
✉ Abdijstraat 40
☎ 014–541001
🕐 Easter holiday, May–Sep: Mon–Sun 2–5; Mar, Apr, Oct: Sun 2–5. Closed Easter
♿ Good
🎫 Cheap
↔ Bobbejaanland (▶ 40)

HOOGSTRATEN ✪

The small town of Hoogstraten is mainly known for the Heilige-Bloedprocessie, a procession that is held on the first and second Sundays after Whitsun. In the centre stands the **St Catharinakerk**, also known as the 'Cathedral of the Kempen'. This church was destroyed by a bombing-raid in 1944. Some five million bricks were used for the reconstruction, which took four years. The interior is particularly striking for its tombs and 16th-century stained glass.

➕ 31D3
St Catharinakerk
☎ 03–3401955
🕐 Apr–Sep: daily 10–5
🍴 Various cafés and restaurants at the Vrijheid (£–£)
🎫 Free

Stained glass windows in St Catharinakerk

KEMPEN NATURE RESERVE ✪✪

Three-quarters of the province of Antwerp is taken up by the Kempen nature reserve. With some 300 walking trails, this reserve is best explored on foot, and there are also cycle routes. The Kalmthoutse Heide is a good starting-point for hikes. In this area of pine forests, moorland with fens and sand dunes, you can explore the short-cuts taken by former smugglers crossing the Dutch and Belgian border.

De Vroente Visitor Centre
➕ 31D3
✉ Putsesteenweg 129
☎ 03–6661228
🕐 Mon–Fri 9–4: Mon and Fri closed noon; Apr–Oct: also Sat–Sun 2–5
🎫 Free

BOBBEJAANLAND, LICHTAART

The Bobbejaanland family theme park is the creation of a Flemish singer named Bobbejaan Schoepen. The park offers more than 50 attractions for children and adults, including the Speedy Bob roller coaster, the Looping and the Whirlwind. The Indianenmuseum displays a collection of utensils and art objects from Native American civilisation. The park hosts daily performances by stars from Belgian show business, including Bobbejaan himself (► 108).

✚ 31E2
✉ Olensesteenweg 45
☎ 014–557811
◷ Days of opening vary every year. Apr and Oct: 10–5 off-season, 9:30–6:30 in peak season
🍴 Expensive
↔ Tongerlo Abbey (► 39)

LIER

✪✪✪

The town of Lier is also called 'Little Bruges' because of its begijnhof (► 6) and canals. One of the most remarkable buildings is the **Zimmertoren**, once described by the Flemish writer Felix Timmermans – one of the many famous people born in Lier – as 'a universe between four walls'. On the outside of the tower is the world-famous 'magic clock', a timepiece with 13 different faces. Don't miss the tower's interior where there is a working planetarium and drive mechanism.

The Begijnhof of Lier is considered to be the most beautiful begijnhof (► 6) of the Kempen. The cobbled streets and renovated cottages with white-washed walls create a peaceful atmosphere. The alleyway called Hemdsmouwken (Shirt-sleeves) derives its name from the fact that the entrance to it is no wider than a shirt-sleeve.

✚ 31D2
Zimmertoren
✉ Zimmerplein 18
☎ 03–4911395
◷ Jan–Feb, Nov–Dec: daily 10–12 and 2–4; Mar, Oct: 10–12 and 2–5; Apr–Sep: 10–12 and 1–6
🍴 Cheap

Above: ride in Bobbejaanland

MECHELEN (MALINES) ✪✪

Mechelen, the religious capital of Belgium, is a city with a rich past. Between 1506 and 1530, Margaret of Austria ruled over the Low Countries from here. The inhabitants of Mechelen are known in Flanders as *maneblussers* (moon-extinguishers). A drunk citizen of Mechelen once raised the alarm because he mistook the moon's glow around the St Romboutskathedraal for fire.

The **St Romboutskathedraal** is among Mechelen's most important attractions. This truncated tower is regarded as one of the most beautiful in Belgium. Fortress-construction expert, Vauban, even called it the 'Eighth Wonder of the World'. The church contains paintings by van Dyck and Artus Quellin. Ludwig van Beethoven's grandfather was once band-master here.

The **Stadhuis** (Town Hall) of Mechelen, at the Grote Markt, comprises three connected buildings and represents different building styles. On the far left is the exuberant Paleis van de Grote Raad. This building with its bay-shaped turrets in the centre was initially intended as the belfry, but the tower was never completed. On the far right is the Lakenhalle, the former cloth hall.

On the edge of the centre stands the splendid **Paleis van Margaretha van Oostenrijk**, the former palace of the governor, Margaret of Austria. This is where she received prominent contemporaries, such as Erasmus and Albrecht Dürer. Emperor Charles V was educated here. The inner courtyard still exudes some of the atmosphere of the most notorious period in the history of Mechelen. Margaret's rooms were on the first floor, above the columns.

🚩 31D2

St Romboutskathedraal
- ✉ Grote Markt
- ☎ 015–218706
- 🕐 Daily 9–12 and 1–5
- ✋ Free
- ❓ The Hanswijk procession through the historic city centre with 2,000 participants takes place every year on the Sunday before Ascension Day

Stadhuis
- ✉ Grote Markt
- ☎ 015–297655
- 🕐 Only guided tours for groups
- 🍴 Restaurant D'Hoogh (££)

Paleis van Margaretha van Oostenrijk
- ✉ Keizerstraat
- ☎ 015–297655
- 🕐 Unrestricted access to inner courtyard; not possible to view building

Stadhuis and Lakenhalle in Mechelen

West Flanders

The soul of Flanders is deeply rooted in the West-Flemish polder landscape. Small villages, tree-lined roads, and church towers on the horizon largely determine the look of the province.

In addition to the rural Scheldt valley and the Westhoek, with its many scars from World War I, West Flanders also boasts a number cities bursting with fine art. In Veurne, the riches from the recent past are still evident in its gables; in Bruges, visitors can imagine themselves to be part of a medieval scene.

West Flanders encompasses Belgium's entire coastal strip. Efforts by towns such as Knokke and Ostend to give the seafront a modern appearance are unfortunately not always successful, but here and there along the boulevards, in the casinos and on the racecourse, the former glory of the *belle époque* lives on.

> ' *Generally speaking, the women are really very good-looking. But they say that those in Bruges are the prettiest.* '
>
> VICTOR HUGO

———————•———————

Left: *Belfry, Bruges*

Winter in Bruges

Bruges

Atmospheric, picturesque and romantic: all these descriptions are applicable to Bruges, *the* tourist attraction of Belgium. This small city, also known as the 'Venice of the North' because of its beautiful canals, draws hundreds of thousands of visitors during the summer months.

In the 15th century, Bruges was a powerful port and trading centre, whose influence reached far into Europe. Its warehouses were packed full of spices and wool, and the art of painting flourished in this centre of culture.

When Het Zwin, the waterway to the sea, silted up, the significance of Bruges declined. The city dozed off into centuries of hibernation. At the end of the 19th century, the publication of Georges Rodenbach's novel *Bruges La Morte* renewed interest in Bruges. British people, in particular, were impressed by its medieval arches and courtyards, its canal houses covered in ivy, and the mighty forts and churches. Bruges is a place where time seems to have stood still.

What to See in Bruges

BASILIEK VAN HET HEILIG BLOED ✪✪

A relic of the Holy Blood is preserved in this basilica. This is a gold-trimmed tube which is alleged to contain a few drops of the blood of Christ – said to have become fluid again on several occasions. Pope Clemens V bestowed the status of 'Official Wonder' upon this phenomenon. During the famous Heilige-Bloedprocessie, a procession held every year on Ascension Day, the relic is carried through the city (➤ 116). The lower part of the basilica, the crypt, contains a 14th-century statue of Our Lady of Mercy.

➕ 50B3 ✉ Burg 13
☎ 050–448686
⏱ Apr–Sep: Mon–Sun 9:30–12 and 2–6; Oct–Mar: Mon–Sun 10–12 and 2–4. Closed Wed noon, 1 Jan, Ascension Day, 25 Dec
🍴 Het Dagelijks Brood (£), Philipstockstraat 21
💶 Cheap
🔁 Stadhuis (➤ 47)

BEGIJNHOF ✪✪

In the spring, when the daffodils are in flower, it is difficult to imagine a more idyllic place than this religious complex by the Minnewater. The Prinselijk Begijnhof Ten Wijngaarde was founded in 1245. Young girls retired from secular life here and led a protected existence, devoted to prayer and meditation. These days, the Begijnhof is inhabited by sisters of the Order of St Benedict. At set times, you will see them hurrying across the courtyard with prayer books under their arms.

🚩 50B3
✉ Wijngaardplein
🚌 Vrijdagmarkt
♿ Reasonable
🔵 Free
↔ Minnewater (➤ 46)

Spring is the best time to visit the Begijnhof in Bruges

BELFORT ✪

The belfry of Bruges dates from the 13th century and dominates the city. Its octagonal upper part was added at the end of the 15th century. The city's statutes used to be announced from the balcony. The 366 steps to the top require good physical fitness, but the views across the city certainly make the climb worthwhile.

🚩 50B3 ✉ Markt 7
☎ 050–448711
🕐 Apr–Sep: Mon–Sun 9:30–5; Oct–Mar: Mon–Sun 9:30–12:30 and 1:30–5
🍴 't Koffieboontje (£), Hallestraat 🚹 Moderate

GROENINGEMUSEUM ✪✪

The Groeningemuseum houses an extensive and magnificent collection of Flemish and Dutch masters. The museum is especially known for its Flemish primitives. The work of these painters, including Hans Memling and Jan van Eyck, is characterised by a lack of perspective. The museum also contains canvases by Pieter Bruegel and Jeroen Bosch, whose *Last Judgement* can be admired here.

🚩 50B3 ✉ Dijver 12
☎ 050–448686
🕐 Apr–Sep: Mon–Sun 9:30–5; Oct–Mar: 9:30–12:30, 2–5. Closed 1 Jan, Ascension Day, 25 Dec, and Tue in winter
🍴 Den Dyver (£££);
♿ Good 🚹 Moderate

45

50B3
Mariastraat 38
050–448711
Apr–Sep: Mon–Sun
9:30–5; Oct–Mar:
Mon–Sun 9:30–12:30
and 1:30–5
Good
Moderate

St Ursula's shrine at
Memling Museum

Opposite: Rozenhoedkaai
is the ideal spot
for photographers

50B3
Between Begijnenvest
and Wijngaardplein
The Bargehuis, just
past the park on the
Bargeweg (££)
Begijnhof (▶ 45)

50B3
Mariastraat
050–345314

MEMLING-MUSEUM

A weekend in Bruges would not be complete without a visit to the Memling Museum. This museum dedicated to the painter Hans Memling (1433–94) contains only six paintings. However, all of them are masterpieces in themselves, striking for their rich detail and realistic portrayal of the subject-matter. The St Ursula shrine, a painted miniature of a Gothic church, is even regarded as one of the most renowned works of Flemish art dating from the 15th century. The museum is housed in a chapel of the former St

Janshospitaal. This hospital was in working use until 1976. Memling is supposed to have been nursed here in the 15th century, after he was wounded in battle as a mercenary of Charles the Bold. In gratitude, the painter donated a number of his canvases to the hospital.

MINNEWATER

The Minnewater is one of the most romantic spots in Bruges. This used to be the mooring place for trading boats and barges from Ghent.

The inhabitants of Bruges have, for centuries, given special care to the swans on these waters. The adoration of swans goes back to the time when Emperor Maximilian of Austria was imprisoned in Bruges and the inhabitants of Bruges beheaded his councillor Pieter Lanchals. Lanchals carried the image of a swan on his coat of arms. When the emperor was set free, he demanded as compensation that the inhabitants of Bruges take care of the swans in the Minnewater. That promise is kept to this day.

ONZE-LIEVE-VROUWEKERK

The 122m-high tower of the Onze-Lieve-Vrouwekerk is built entirely of brick and the church houses a number of famous art works, both paintings and sculptures such as the *Virgin and Child*, hewn from white marble and one of Michelangelo's masterpieces. The 16th-century tombs of Charles the Bold and Mary of Burgundy are certainly worth viewing. The question as to whether Charles is actually buried in the cathedral remains unanswered. Some say that after the battle near Nancy, it was impossible to identify the body, while others believe it was taken to Luxembourg, where it remained for three years.

ROZENHOEDKAAI ✪✪

The Rozenhoedkaai is considered to be one of the most picturesque spots in Bruges. The view of the water, the canal houses covered in ivy and the silhouette of the belfry ensure that there is nearly always someone with a camera taking pictures here. During a boat trip on the canals – an absolute must – you can admire this beautiful sight from the water.

🕐 Apr–Sep: Mon–Sun 10–11:30 and 2:30–5; Oct–Mar: Mon–Sun 10–11:30 and 2:30–4:30; Sat until 4. Closed Sun, holidays
♿ Good 👌 Cheap

✚ 50B3
✉ Rozenhoedkaai
🍴 Restaurants on Eekhoutstraat and Vismarkt, such as Den Eeckhoute (££) and De Visscherie (£)
↔ Basiliek van het Heilig Bloed (➤ 44)

STADHUIS ✪✪

Bruges Town Hall is one of the oldest in the Low Countries. Built between 1376 and 1420, this building was the site of the first meeting of the States-General of the Low Countries. The gable shows statues of the various counts of Flanders while the vertical lines, accentuated by the pointed turrets and elongated arched windows, are also striking.

On the first floor of the Stadhuis is a large and splendid Gothic hall with an elegant wooden hanging vault dating from between 1385 and 1402. The murals portray scenes from the history of the city.

✚ 50B3 ✉ Burg 12
☎ 050–448686
🕐 Apr–Sep: Mon–Sun 9:30–5; Oct–Mar: Mon–Sun 9:30–12:30 and 2–5
♿ Good 👌 Moderate (combined ticket with Brugse Vrije Renaissance room)
↔ Basiliek van het Heilig Bloed (➤ 44)

What to See in West Flanders

BLANKENBERGE ⭐

Blankenberge in the summer offers every kind of modern seaside entertainment, from beach volleyball tournaments to the now ubiquitous Miss Wet T-shirt competition. The **pier**, Blankenberge's showpiece built in 1933, gives the seafront a stately appearance that contrasts with the modern apartment blocks. At the end of the pier you'll find the Aquarama, a collection of aquariums with tropical fish, minerals and shells.

✚ 50B3

Pier
✉ Pier–Zeedijk
☎ 050–412940
🕐 Mar–Jun and 1–12 Sep: Mon–Sun 11–6; Jul, Aug: Mon–Sun 10–9; 13 Sep–7 Nov: Sat–Sun 11–6
💷 Moderate

The **Lustige Velodrome** (➤ 109), also known as Louis' track, is a wooden cycling track, where every bicycle has a quirk. Some bicycles have oval wheels, others have their handlebars the wrong way round and others again suffer from a wobbly saddle. It is a hilarious sight to see the cyclists bumping about the track or if you are brave, why not have a go yourself. Have the camera ready!

Lustige Velodrome
✉ Next to the pier
☎ 050–427020
🕐 Easter–15 Sep: Mon–Sun 9–6
🍴 De La Providence (£), Zeedijk 191
💷 Cheap

DAMME ⭐⭐

Near Bruges is the picturesque town of Damme. The medieval town centre, with its white-washed houses and elegant Gothic Town Hall, reveals a relatively recent prosperity. The most noteworthy building is the **Onze-Lieve-Vrouwekerk**, built in the 14th century. In good weather, the tower offers magnificent views across the area and when the skies are clear, you can even see across the Dutch border.

Onze-Lieve-Vrouwekerk
✚ 30B3
✉ Kerkstraat
☎ 050–353319
🕐 Easter and May–Sep: 10–12 and 2:30–5:30
🍴 Brasserie 't Hemeltje (£)
💷 Cheap

Damme is the 'birthplace' of Till Eulenspiegel. In the novel of the same name by Charles de Koster, Till, together with his inseparable companion Lamme Goedzak, is constantly obstructing the Spanish Inquisition.

Nowadays, Lamme Goedzak is the name of a small boat which sails across the Damse Vaart waterway to Bruges five times a day. This trip is certainly worth making. Behind the poplar-lined shores there lies a wide polder landscape. Beside the Damse Vaart stands the photogenic Schellemolen, a provincial windmill dating from 1867.

DIKSMUIDE ✪✪

Diksmuide had to be rebuilt after World War I and the original plans were faithfully followed, resulting in some pleasant areas, for example around the Grote Markt.

In the vicinity of Diksmuide, at the German cemetery near Vladslo, stands one of the most poignant statues to remind us of the horrors of World War I: *Grieving Parents* by the expressionist sculptress Käthe Kollwitz. Her son, who perished in World War I, lies buried in this cemetery. Other reminders of the war are also to be found nearby (► 16).

Lamme Goedzak
☎ 050–353319
🕐 Apr–Sep: Mon–Sun.
 Departure times Damme:
 9:15, 11, 1, 3 and 5:20.
 Departure times Bruges:
 10, 12, 2, 4:20. Landing
 stage Noorweegse
 Kaai 18
✋ Moderate
❓ Trip takes 35 minutes

✚ 50A2
✉ 3.5km (2 miles) northeast
 of Diksmuide
♿ Good ↔ Veurne (► 56)

Opposite: *Lustige Velodrome, cycling for the skillful*

Damse Vaart between Damme and Bruges

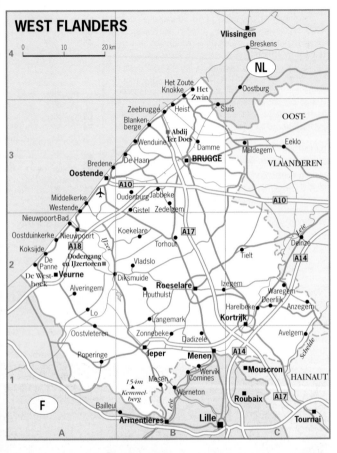

WEST FLANDERS

0   10   20 km

Vlissingen
Breskens
NL
Het Zoute
Knokke • Het
Zwin • Oostburg
Zeebrugge • Heist   Sluis   **OOST-**
Blanken-
berge   **Abdij**
• Wenduine   **Ter Does**
Damme   Eeklo
Bredene   De Haan   **BRUGGE**   Maldegem
Oostende   **VLAANDEREN**
A10
Middelkerke   Oudenburg Jabbeke   **A10**
Westende   • Gistel Zedelgem
Nieuwpoort-Bad
Koekelare   **A17**
Oostduinkerke • Nieuwpoort   Deinze
Koksijde   **A18**   Torhout   **A14**
• De   **Dodengang**   Tielt
Panne   **en IJzertoren** ■   Vladslo
De West-   ■ **Veurne**   Diksmuide   **Roeselare** ■   Izegem
hoek   Alveringem   Houthulst   Waregem
Deerlijk Anzegem
Lo   Harelbeke   **Kortrijk**
Oostvleteren   Langemark
Zonnebeke   Avelgem
Poperinge   Dadizele
Ieper   **Menen**   **A14**
154m   Mesen   Wervik   ■**Mouscron**   **HAINAUT**
Kemmel-   Comines
F   berg   Warneton   **Roubaix**   **A17**
Bailleul
Armentières   **Lille**   Tournai

A   B   C

✚ 50B1

Flanders Fields Museum

✉ Grote Markt 34

☎ 057–228584

🕐 Apr–Sep: Mon–Sun 10–6;
Oct–Mar: Tue–Sun 10–5.
Closed first 3 weeks after
Christmas holiday

♿ Good   🍴 Moderate

IEPER (YPRES)   ❋❋❋

Ieper once was one of the proud capitals of the textile industry. The Lakenhalle was the largest civil building project of the 19th century.

Flanders Fields Museum has been housed here since Easter 1998. The museum gives an incisive picture of the battle of attrition fought on both sides of the notorious Ypres Salient (bulge), the front line around Ieper. Visitors can follow the course of the battle by means of interactive media, such as CD-ROM, video projections and computers. The museum pays particular attention to eye-witness accounts.

Ieper is also known as the 'Hiroshima of World War I': for four years, the city was in the front line and was largely destroyed. Although a significant part of the centre has been restored, the region still bears the scars of the horrors of the 'Great War', such as the 147 military cemeteries around the city. On the edge of the city centre stands the **Menenpoort**, the Menin Gate war memorial, erected in memory of more than 250,000 British soldiers who died here. As a homage to the dead, a 'Last Post' has been sounded under the porch every night at 8PM since 1928.

> ## DID YOU KNOW?
>
> In the Middle Ages, live cats were regularly thrown down from the Belfry in Ieper, a ritual which was supposed to challenge the devil. These days, the inhabitants use the soft-toy variety.

JABBEKE ✪

The **Provinciaal Museum Constant Permeke** is housed in the 'Vier Winden', the former workshop and living quarters of the painter and sculptor, Permeke. This expressionist painter became known particularly for his rough sketches of Flemish farming life. In addition to 80 of his paintings and sketches, the museum contains almost all his sculptures.

Menenpoort

✉ East of the Grote Markt, accessible via the Meensestraat

🕐 'Last Post': every evening at 8PM

Below: *Lakenhalle, Ieper*

✚ 50B3

Provinciaal Museum Constant Permeke

✉ Gistelsteenweg 341

☎ 050–811288

🕐 Apr–Sep: Tue–Sun 10– 12:30 and 1:30–6; Oct– Mar: Tue– Sun 10–12:30 and 1:30–5

🚩 50C2

Begijnhof

✉ Between the St
Maartenskerk and
O.-L.-Vrouwekerk

☎ 056–239371

🕐 Sunrise–sunset:
Begijnhofmuseum
15 Mar–1 Jan: Tue–Thu
2:30–5:30, weekend
10–12 and 2:30–5:30

♿ Good

♨ Free

↔ Flemish Ardennes (➤ 25)

Belfort

✉ Grote Markt

🍴 Various cafés and
restaurants in and around
the Grote Markt, such as
den Engel (£) and Arte (£)

🚇 NMBS station a 5 min.
walk from Grote Markt
(via Doorniksestraat)

♿ None

Broeltorens

✉ Broelkaai

Above: *the Broeltorens
on the shores of the River
Leie*
Above right: *Kalle and
Manten, the most famous
bell-ringers in Flanders*

KORTRIJK (COURTRAI) ✪✪

The commercial city of Kortrijk, on the River Leie, has many buildings which are a reminder of its rich past. In the middle of the busy city centre, the **Begijnhof** offers you an oasis of peace. The Flemish writer Felix Timmermans once wrote of this religious place: 'The walls lean forward, weary of standing for so many centuries'.

It consists of 40 white-washed baroque cottages and the house of the former mother superior, which is now a museum. The chapel of Onze-Lieve-Vrouw-ter-Sneeuw is also well worth a visit.

The **Belfort** of Kortrijk is a remnant of the Lakenhallen (cloth halls), which were built in the Middle Ages. The statues of the bell-ringers Manten (Armand) and Kalle (Katelijne) stand in the ivy-covered tower. These two figures have enabled the clocks to resound across the city as far back as the 14th century. The statues were stolen by the French in 1382, taken to Dijon, and finally replaced by new ones in 1961.

On the shores of the Leie, two impressive medieval towers rise up, which are linked by a bridge. The southern of the **Broeltorens**, the Speyetoren built in the 12th century, is part of the enclosure of the count's castle. The northern Inghelborchttoren was erected later for the defence of the city.

KNOKKE-HEIST ✪

At present, Knokke presents itself mainly as a shopping city. Together with the adjacent town of Heist, this seaside resort has no less than 1,500 shops, exclusive boutiques and galleries. The pivot of sophisticated nightlife is the **casino**, which displays works of art by Delvaux, Zadkine and Keith Haring. The casino's main feature is the monumental chandelier in the hall, made from Venetian crystal. It weighs more than 7 tonnes and is apparently the largest chandelier in the world.

On the edge of Knokke is the **Vlindertuin**. This butterfly garden contains a large number of colourful butterflies with bright patterns. The butterflies are housed in a large conservatory, where the conditions of a tropical rain forest have been emulated as closely as possible. The cocoons from which the butterflies emerge are brought in from Guernsey, which has a temperate climate thanks to the warm Gulf Stream.

Casino
🔲 50B3/4
✉ Zeedijk Albertstrand 507
☎ 050–630505
🍽 Various restaurants on the Albertstrand, such as Les Flots Bleus (££)
♿ Good
🔄 Het Zwin (► 26)

Vlindertuin
🔲 50B4
✉ Bronlaan 14
☎ 050–610472
🕐 21 Mar–1st weekend in Oct: Mon–Sun 10–5:30
🚌 Bronlaan (bus 788 from NMBS station)
♿ Good
💰 Moderate

The Paul Delvaux Museum in Koksijde

KOKSIJDE ✪✪

In a villa in the artists' quarter of St Idesbald is the largest collection of paintings by the surrealist painter Paul Delvaux. The **Paul Delvaux Museum** clearly shows how much the painter was fascinated by trams, trains and shunting yards. These constantly recur in his dreamscapes, as do partying and drinking skeletons and naked women. These women, who strongly resemble classical Roman statues, caused much uproar among the bourgeoisie at the time (mid-20th century).

Paul Delvaux Museum
🔲 50A2
✉ Delvauxlaan 42
☎ 058–521229
🕐 Apr–Sep: Tue–Sun 10:30–6:30; Jul–Aug: also Mon; Oct–Dec: closes 5:30
🍽 Good brasserie
♿ Moderate
🔄 De Panne (► 56)

53

Food and Drink

The Flemish are Epicureans who love to wine and dine. This is clearly reflected in the cuisine. It would not be over the top to spend an entire evening enjoying a good dinner.

More than 750 native types of beer are brewed in Belgium

Flemish Cuisine

In addition to the traditional meat and fish dishes inspired by French cuisine, many restaurants serve typically Flemish dishes, such as *paling in het groe*, eel in a sauce of fresh green herbs, or *waterzooi*, a filling soup of chicken cooked in stock and finished with eggs and cream.

Hutsepot met gebraden haring, a stew with baked herring, is also famous, as is Flemish rabbit – rabbit stewed in a mixture of red wine, dark beer, thyme, laurel and mustard. Many towns and regions have their own specialities, such as *koekoek*, a breed of hen which is a popular dish around Mechelen, and *stoemp*, potato puree with vegetables, which is often on the menu in Brussels.

Relaxing on one of many city terraces

Friet (Chips)

Away from the restaurant, the paper cone filled with chips (*friet*) is still a classic Flemish snack. In The Netherlands, the term 'Flemish fries' has almost the status of a quality mark. The majority of chip shops in Belgium still make their fries from real potatoes as opposed to the flour-based mixture favoured by most fast-food chains.

Cheese

Those who think that only France and The Netherlands produce special cheeses will be pleasantly surprised in Flanders. There are a considerable number of regional specialities, such as *Faymonville* from Brussels, the piquant *Passendale* or *Pelgrim*, which tastes slightly like Emmenthal. As is the case with many beers, there are a number of cheeses which originate from the abbeys. At the gates of Westmalle Abbey, for example, you can buy a delicious Trappist cheese.

Beer

No other region in the world has a greater variety of beers than Flanders (although many English, Scots and Irish would dispute this). More than 750 native beers are brewed in Belgium. The names of the beers often warn of the dangers of excessive consumption, but 'real' beer drinkers would not flinch from a *Houten Kop* (wooden head), a *Mort Subite* (instant death) or a *Moeder Overste* (Reverend Mother).

Although Belgium produces a number of excellent pilseners (such as Stella Artois, Maes and Jupiler), the term 'Belgian beer' normally refers to the slightly heavier, darker types of beer, of which Palm and De Koninck are the best known abroad.

Belgium's most popular export product: chocolates

Other popular beers are Hoegaarden, Duvel, Verboden Vrucht, Gueuze and Kriek. Gueuze and Kriek beers are made by means of a spontaneous fermentation process: no yeast is added during preparation.

Each beer is poured into its own kind of glass. Kwak, which is served in a flask-shaped glass with a narrow neck is notorious for spilling during over-enthusiastic consumption. According to those in the know, Kwak owes its name to the sound made when it is drunk from this glass.

Chocolate and Waffles

Belgium is famous for its chocolate. Chocolates (*pralines*, as the Belgians call them) are sold on every street corner. Other sweet things are also popular in Flanders. The Brussels waffle is an emblem, as are the *Lierse vlaaikens* (fruit flans) and the *Geraardsbergse mattentaart*, a tart made from quark, buttermilk and almonds.

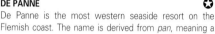

| 50A2 |
| West of the village centre and the monument for King Leopold, in the direction of the French border |
| Koksijde (► 53) |
| Five marked walking routes are set out in the Westhoek, which vary in length from 1.7 to 7km (1–4 miles) |

'The Sahara', an area of dunes near De Panne

| 50A2 |
| Diksmuide (► 16 and 49) |

Stadhuis
| Grote Markt 27 |
| 058–330531 |
| Guided tours from Apr–Sep: 11, 2, 3 and 4:30; Oct–Mar: 11 and 3 |
| Few |
| Cheap |

St Walburgakerk
| St Walburgapark |
| Apr–Sep: Mon–Sun 10–6 |
| Various café-restaurants in the Grote Markt, such as De Beurs, Flandria and Ibis (£) |
| Free |

DE PANNE ⭐

De Panne is the most western seaside resort on the Flemish coast. The name is derived from *pan*, meaning a bowl-shaped plateau or dune valley. The town is partly surrounded by a beautiful nature reserve called the Westhoek. In the middle of this area lies a large sandy plain known as 'the Sahara' (► 12). During hot summers, when the heat lingers between the dips in the dunes, the conditions there can seem a little desert-like.

VEURNE ⭐⭐

The atmospheric town of Veurne is also known as 'the Spanish city'. Spanish garrisons were posted here during the Habsburg occupation. Many beautiful houses and monuments, such as the Spanish Pavilion, date from this period. The market square is one of the best preserved in Flanders. It is surrounded by buildings in rural Renaissance style, such as the **Stadhuis** (Town Hall) with its magnificent blue-stone lower facade and the two elegant gables decorated with gold.

Behind the Town Hall is the **St Walburgakerk**, a church with a chequered history. In 1099 Count Robert II of Flanders returned from the crusades with a piece of the Holy Cross. His ship was caught in a storm and in desperation, he promised to donate the relic to the very first church he came across. This happened to be the St Walburgakerk. Since that time, the relic has been in a special shrine in the right-hand aisle of the church.

HET ZWIN (► 26, TOP TEN)

A Drive Through West Flanders

This tour leads past World War I trenches.

From Bruge (➤ 44) take the N367 to Jabbeke and Gistel. Near the hamlet of St Pieterkapelle, 7.5km (4.5 miles) past Gistel, turn left in the direction of Diksmuide (N369). After 8km (5 miles), turn left at Beerst and 1.5km (1 mile) further on, turn right at Hoograad in the direction of Vladslo.

At the German war cemetery near Vladslo stands one of the most poignant memorials from World War I, *Grieving Parents* by the German sculptress Käthe Kollwitz (➤ 49).

From Vladslo, take the N35, via Essen, to Diksmuide.

Along the River IJzer, just east of Diksmuide, are two impressive reminders of World War I, the Dodengang and the IJzertoren (➤ 16).

From Diksmuide (➤ 16, 49), take the N35 in the direction of Veurne (➤ 56). After 1.5km (1 mile), turn left onto the N364 to Lo-Reninge, where you turn left to Reninge 5km (3 miles) further on. Turn right here towards Vleteren, where you take the N8 to Ieper.

A large part of Ieper was destroyed during World War I (➤ 50). After the war, the city was rebuilt. The Flanders Fields Museum (➤ 50) is housed in the magnificent Lakenhalle.

Take the N365 to Mesen, after 1km (just over half a mile) turn right onto the N331 to Kemmel.

Kemmel is one of the municipalities of Heuvelland (➤ 12), an undulating region where some 20 hills offer unique views. This is beautiful walking country.

From Kemmel, follow the signs for Kemmelberg. In Loker, take the N373 in the direction of Poperinge. Past Reningelst the road merges into the N304. At Poperinge, take the N321 towards Vleteren, where you take the N8 in the direction of Veurne. Drive back to Bruges via the A18.

Begijnhof, Diksmuide

Distance
150km (93 miles)

Start/end point
Brugge
✚ 50B3

Time
6 hours

Lunch
In 't Klein Stadhuis (£)
🖂 Grote Markt, Ieper

Grieving Parents: *an indictment against the horrors of World War I*

East Flanders

From the undulating Flemish Ardennes to the polder landscape of Meetjesland: the landscape of East Flanders is more varied than that of any other part of the region. Rural areas, such as the picturesque Leiestreek (► 20), alternate with historically interesting towns such as Oudenaarde (► 66), Dendermonde (► 65) and Aalst (► 64). Traditions and folklore are much valued in this province of which Ghent (► 60–63) is the capital in every respect: historically, economically and culturally.

The old capital of Flanders, Ghent, is still considered by many to be the most attractive city in the country. For lovers of culture as well as for Burgundian epicureans it is a destination not to be missed.

> *'I believe that in the whole of Christianity you will not find a city which can stand up to a comparison with Ghent.'*

ERASMUS

———————•———————

Left: *giants' procession in Dendermonde*

*The Ghent festivals
attract hundreds of
thousands of visitors
every year*

Ghent

**The capital of East Flanders is a bustling city,
with an historic centre where the past is
clearly still present. There is no other place
with so many monuments in such a small
area. The St Baafskathedraal, the Belfort
and the magnificent guild houses along the
Graslei and Korenlei are reminders of the
time when, after Paris, Ghent was the most
important city in Europe.**

There is also a clear sense of the present here. As a
university city, Ghent is naturally very lively, but it is also the
second seaport in the country and therefore of considerable
economic importance to the region.

The River Leie runs through Ghent's city centre and its
quaysides, where the wool ships from England used to
moor, are a perfect starting point for a walk among the many
guild houses and cafés.

What to See in Ghent

BELFORT   ✪✪

Opposite the entrance to the St Baafskathedraal is the
proud Belfort. The 95m-high tower of this belfry was for a
long time the symbol of the power of the guilds. The Belfort
was built in 1300. The upper gallery offers a splendid view
across the city and guards used to keep watch for fire from
this look-out point.

The 15th-century Gothic Lakenhalle (cloth-makers' hall),
next to the belfry, was a place where cloth and wool
merchants gathered to trade and to solve disputes.

➕ 64B2
✉ Botermarkt 17
☎ 09-2330772
🕐 14 Mar–11 Nov: daily
10–1, 2–6. Closed
11 Jul
♿ Few
🖐 Cheap
↔ St Baafskathedraal
(➤ 23)

GRASLEI AND KORENLEI ✪✪✪

The Graslei and Korenlei are undoubtedly the most beautiful canals in Ghent, lined by a unique succession of guild houses which are reflected in the water of the Leie. In the Middle Ages, the old port of Ghent was situated here.

The different decorative gables of the guild houses clearly show the various building styles which were in vogue at the time: Romanesque, Gothic and Renaissance. Note the fine guild house belonging to the *Vrije Schippers* (Free Skippers) at Graslei 14, with the image of a sailing ship above the entrance. The Toll House at No. 11, a fine example of Flemish Renaissance style, is the smallest house in the city.

🚩 64B2
✉ Gras- and Korenlei
🍴 Various cafés and restaurants, such as Het Spijker on the Graslei (£)
🚌 Korenmarkt, bus/tram 1, 10, 11, 12, 13
↔ St Michielsbrug (➤ 62)

GRAVENSTEEN ✪✪✪

The Gravensteen was built in 1180 by Philip of Alsace, Count of Flanders. This rather grim looking fort was inspired by crusaders' forts in Syria. Over the centuries, the Gravensteen has been used for various purposes, including a court of law and a cotton mill. A visit to the castle offers an opportunity to admire the massive fortified and loopholed walls. The Gravensteen also houses a collection of instruments of torture and execution. These dungeons and torture chambers clearly show that legal authorities in the Middle Ages had very effective methods of obtaining confessions.

🚩 64B2
✉ St Veerleplein
☎ 09–2259306
🕐 Apr–Sep: daily 9–6; Oct–Mar: daily 9–5. Closed 25–26 Dec, 1–2 Jan
🎫 Moderate

Below: *the Graslei, one of the most beautiful canals in Ghent*

PATERSHOL ✪✪

The district of Patershol consists of an attractive network of small streets and alleyways. It was once a smart neighbourhood, but in the 19th century became one of the poorest parts of the city.

In the 1980s, the district, which owes its name to a small tunnel under the Carmelites' monastery, was extensively renovated. Fortunately, its most important features, the small scale of the buildings and the medieval street plan, were preserved in the process. Patershol now has a good choice of cafés and restaurants.

🚩 64B2
✉ Northeast of the Gravensteen, between the Kraanlei and the Lange Steenstraat
🍴 Numerous cafés and restaurants, such as De Drie Biggetjes in the Zeugsteeg (££) and Amadeus on the Plotersgracht (£)
🚌 Gravensteen bus/tram 1, 10, 11, 12, 13, 40, 42
❓ Patershol festivities, mid-August
↔ Vrijdagsmarkt (➤ 63)

The medieval street plan of the Patershol district is still largely intact

ST BAAFSKATHEDRAAL (➤ 23, TOP TEN)

ST MICHIELSBRUG ✪✪✪

The monumental St Michielsbrug bridge is especially famous for its stunning view. From the bridge you can see all three towers of Ghent; the St Niklaaskerk, the Belfort (belfry) and the St Baafskathedraal. To the left are the Graslei and Korenlei, the two most beautiful canals in Ghent (➤ 61).

🚩 64B2
✉ Between Korenmarkt and St Michielsplein
🚌 Korenmarkt bus/tram 1, 10, 11, 12, 13
↔ Gras- and Korenlei (➤ 61)

DID YOU KNOW?

Ghent has an important reputation as a city of flowers. The *Floraliën*, which are held every five years, draw tens of thousands of visitors (➤ 114). The flower-growers are concentrated mainly around Lochristi, northeast of Ghent.

S.M.A.K.

In the Citadelpark, on the south side of the city centre, stands the recently re-opened Stedelijk Museum voor Actuele Kunst (S.M.A.K.). This museum is an important showcase for developments in contemporary art. Its curator Jan Hoet is also known outside Flanders because of his much-discussed and controversial exhibitions. During the exhibition *Over the Edges* (Spring 2000), for example, pedestrians in the Korenlei were witness to a week-long 'row', with a plate being thrown out of a window every five minutes. The S.M.A.K. collection includes work by Belgian and international artists, such as Panamarenko, Bacon and Beuys.

🕂 64B2
✉ Citadelpark
☎ 09–2211703
🕐 Tue–Sun 10–6. Closed 25–26 Dec, 1–2 Jan
🖐 Few

VRIJDAGMARKT

The Vrijdagmarkt square, with its many cafés and a small bird market held on Sundays, has regularly been the scene of political fighting over the past centuries. In the middle of the square stands the statue of Jacob van Artevelde, a 14th-century democratic revolutionary, who presented himself as leader of the wool weavers and later united the Flemish cities as an ally of England.

Next to the square stands the Dulle Griet ('Mad Meg'), a 15th-century cannon weighing no less than 16,000kg. Only one cannonball has ever been fired with this weapon; once in operation, it posed more of a danger to the operator than to the enemy.

🕂 64B2
✉ Vrijdagmarkt and Groot Kanonplein
🍴 Numerous cafés and restaurants, such as Taverne Keizershof (£) on the Vrijdagmarkt and De Hel (££) on the Kraanlei
🚌 St Jacobs bus/tram 3, 16, 19
↔ Patershol (► 62)

Vrijdagmarkt with the statue of Jacob van Artevelde

What to See in East Flanders

AALST ⊙⊙

The history of the town of Aalst is dominated by its two most famous inhabitants. In the Grote Markt stands the statue of Dirk Martens. Martens introduced the art of book printing to the southern Netherlands, which stimulated the distribution of new ideas such as humanism.

Aalst was also the home town of Adolf Daens. This socially active priest endeavoured to improve the conditions of exploited textile workers at the end of the 19th century. The Grote Markt boasts a number of striking buildings, including the oldest *Schepenhuis* (shipping house) in the Low Countries. This elegantly restored building, which was completed in 1225, was built in Scheldt-Gothic style. The gable bears the motto of Philip II: *Nec spe, nec metu* (Neither through hope, nor through fear). The Belfort next to the *Schepenhuis* dates from the 15th century. During the Monday of the annual carnival, onions are thrown from this belfry.

✚ 64C1
✉ 25km (15.5 miles) southeast of Ghent
☎ 053–732270
🍴 Some cafés serving food around the Grote Markt (£) and the Borse van Amsterdam (£££)
🚌 NMBS Aalst
↔ Dendermonde (► 65)

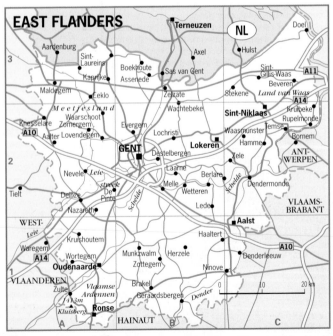

DENDERMONDE ✪✪✪

Dendermonde is known as the town of Ros Beiaard. According to legend, this horse helped the sons of Amyon, Lord of Dendermonde, to escape from the soldiers of Charles V several times. Eventually, the horse was drowned in the Scheldt by order of the Emperor. The story is re-enacted every ten years during the **Ros Beiaard-ommegang**. This procession includes three giants and 800 costumed participants.

The town of Dendermonde is situated where the River Dender flows into the Scheldt and it is especially worth a visit to see the buildings around the **Grote Markt**. The most striking of these is the former Lakenhalle, which now houses the Town Hall.

Both the Lakenhalle and the belfry were built in the 14th century. Close to the Grote Markt stands the Gothic Onze-Lieve-Vrouwekerk. Inside the church is a number of interesting paintings by David Teniers and Antoon van Dyck.

GERAARDSBERGEN ✪✪

Geraardsbergen is especially known for the *Muur* (the 'wall'), notorious amongst racing cyclists. This steep stretch of cobbled road is the place of the final in the annual Ronde van Vlaanderen, the most important cycling event in the country's sporting calendar (➤ 116). Cycling enthusiasts donning sport kits regularly pull themselves up, huffing and puffing, from the foot of the hill in order to be photographed triumphant at the top.

The track across the *Muur* leads to the top of the 110m-high Oudenberg. This is where the annual pretzel-throwing takes place – an event that is preceded by a folkloristic procession with many figures from the town's history. When they reach the highest point, prominent citizens from Geraardsbergen drink wine from a silver beaker containing live fish. As a reward, they are allowed to bombard the spectators with pretzels (➤ 116).

🟪 64C2
🔲 Aalst (➤ 64)

Ros Beiaard-ommegang
🔲 In and around Grote Markt
🕐 Next held in 2010. There is also an annual procession with three guild giants, Thursday after the fourth Sunday in August
☎ 052–213956

Grote Markt
🔲 Grote Markt
☎ 052–213956
🕐 Mon–Fri 10–12, 2–4; Sun and holidays: 10–12, 2–4:30; Easter to end-Sep and school holidays also Sat 10–12, 2–4:30
♿ None 🔲 Free

🟪 64B1
🔲 30km (18 miles) south of Ghent
☎ 054–414121
🍴 Various cafés around the Grote Markt (£)
♿ None
🔄 Flemish Ardennes (➤ 25)
❓ Pretzel-throwing takes place every year on the last Sunday of Feb

---

Above: *once every ten years, the Ros Beiaard-ommegang takes place in Dendermonde*

64A1

✉ Grote Markt

☎ 055-317251

🕐 Guided tours: Mon–Fri 11, 2 and 3:30, Sat–Sun 2 and 3:30

♿ None

🍴 Few

↔ Flemish Ardennes (▶ 25)

64C2

✉ 15km (9 miles) southwest of Antwerp

☎ 03-7741915

🚌 Bus from Antwerp

↔ Antwerp (▶ 30)

Below: St Niklaas Town Hall

64C2

Mercator Museum

✉ Zamanstraat 49

☎ 03-7772942

🕐 Tue–Sat 2–5, Sun 10–5. Closed 25–26 Dec, 1–2 Jan.

♿ Good 🍴 Few

OUDENAARDE ✪✪

Oudenaarde is, after Ghent, the most important city of art in East Flanders. The Grote Markt is lined with impressive, if somewhat neglected Renaissance buildings. The city's showpiece is the Town Hall in late-Gothic Brabant style, one of the most beautiful in Flanders. The gilded statue at the top of the Belfort tower represents Hanske de Krijger, a legendary figure who protected the city in bad times.

The Romanesque Lakenhalle, next to the Town Hall, dates from the 13th century and contains the famous verdures, tapestries which made Oudenaarde world-famous in the 17th century. The tapestries derive their name from their verdant (greenish-blue) colour.

RUPELMONDE ✪

Follow the Scheldt downstream from Antwerp and you soon come to Rupelmonde. The population of this small lively village was, until fairly recently, dependent on fishing for its livelihood. The tides made it possible for the fish to swim a long way up the River Scheldt from the North Sea. The fishermen's district of Schelleke is a reminder of that time. On the shores of the Scheldt stands the Gravenkasteel, a moated fortress where the cartographer Mercator was born in 1512.

ST NIKLAAS ✪

The town of St Niklaas prides itself on having Belgium's largest market square. There are also a number of historical buildings here, such as the neo-Gothic Town Hall. The size of the square ensures that the town regularly hosts large-scale events, such as the peace festivities: a massive hot-air balloon display which takes place every year at the beginning of September. In good weather, this is guaranteed to be a very colourful event.

The **Mercator Museum** is devoted to the cartographer Mercator, who was born in this region. The museum collection includes a first edition of Mercator's Atlas and a globe dating from 1541.

The category of curious museums would not be complete without the inclusion of the historic Pijp en Tabaksmuseum (Pipe and Tobacco Museum) at Regentiestraat 29. The entrance features the largest cigar in the world, an object no less than 6m long and weighing some 450kg. For the enthusiast!

FLEMISH ARDENNES (▶ 25, TOP TEN)

Drive Through the Flemish Ardennes

From Aalst (▶ 64), take the N460 in the direction of Haaltert. After 6.5km (4 miles), turn right towards Aaigem. At Opaaigem, 3.5km (2 miles) further on, turn left to Herzele, where you continue on the road in the direction of Zottegem.

You are now entering the Flemish Ardennes (▶ 25), a region with a strong rural character, which is popular with racing cycle enthusiasts and walkers because of its constantly rolling hills. The landscape is characterised by small villages, white-washed farmsteads and groups of pollarded willows.

From Zottegem, take the N454 in the direction of Oudenaarde. Via Strijpen you reach Kouteren after some 5.5km (3.5 miles), where you turn right towards Zwalm (▶ 25).

Zwalm is the name of a group of villages around the Zwalm stream. The green valley on both sides of the stream is considered to be one of the most beautiful places in Flanders.

Via St Denijs–Boekel and St Blasius–Boekel, return to the N454, following it as far as Ronse. Now take the N36 to Kluisbergen. After 5km (3 miles), the Kluisbos is on your left–hand side.

The Kluisbos is a long strip of woodland which runs parallel to the 141m-high Kluisberg. The French-Dutch linguistic divide falls directly south of this wood.

Follow the N36 past Berchem. Immediately after crossing the Scheldt, turn right on to the N453 to Oudenaarde.

The historic centre of Oudenaarde (▶ 66), East Flanders' second city of art, is definitely worth a visit.

Take the N8 to Geraardsbergen.

Via the *Muur* (the 'wall') of Geraardsbergen (▶ 65, 116), notorious amongst racing cyclists and one of the few remaining sections of cobbled road, climb the Oudenberg, which offers splendid views across the surrounding area.

Via Onkerzele, take the local road to Ninove and then take the N45 to Aalst (▶ 64).

Lengte
130km (80 miles)

Time
5 hours

Start/end point
Aalst
➕ 64C1

Lunch
The Look (££)
✉ Priestersstraat 6, Ronse
☎ 055–212148

Onze-Lieve-Vrouwekerk on the Oudenberg at the top of Geraardsbergen Muur

In the Know

If you would like to become acquainted with the culture of Flanders or attempt a picture of daily life, here are some ideas:

10 Local Customs

Watch one of the many processions, such as the Hanswijkprocessie in Mechelen.

Rummage around a flea market in search of a second-hand comic book, reproduction or antique cupboard.

After church on Sunday, go to the village café and order a *pintje*.

Forget the clock. Take your time for everything you see and do. There is no need to rush here.

Watch a pigeon race and admire the dedication with which pigeon breeders coach their champions.

Wander round a funfair, have a go at the try-your-strength machine or hit the bull's-eye in the shooting gallery.

Enjoy good cuisine and a full wine-cellar in one of the restaurants.

Go to a cycle race. Daub the name of a racing cyclist on the road at night and support your favourite cyclist by the roadside the next day.

Choose a terrace café in the Grand-Place in Brussels (➤ 17) and watch the world go by. Jean Cocteau once described this square as 'the most beautiful theatre in the world'.

Rent a beach hut and enjoy your own private space on a North Sea beach.

10 Good Places to Have Lunch

Den Ommeganck (£)
✉ Grote Markt 18, Dendermonde
☎ 052–213408

Faits Divers (££)
✉ Korenmarkt 31, Ghent
☎ 09–2330601

Le Pain Quotidien (£–££)
✉ Grote Zavel 11, Brussels
☎ 02–5135154

The Look (££)
✉ Priesterstraat 6, Ronse ☎ 055–212148

Zuiderterras (££)
✉ Ernest van Dijckkaai 37, Antwerp
☎ 03–2341275

Ramberg Hof (£££)
✉ Naamsestraat 60, Leuven ☎ 016–293272

De Foyer (£–££)
✉ Komedieplaats 18 (Bourlaschouwburg), Antwerp ☎ 03–2335517

Se@Site (££)
Meat and fish specialities in modern decor.
✉ Alfons Pieterslaan 86, Ostend ☎ 059–568818

Toermalijn (£–££)
Small vegetarian restaurant.
✉ Coupure 29A, Bruges
☎ 050–340194

Herberg 'De Swaen' (££)
Regional dishes in a pub dating from 1742.
✉ Kinkenberg 188, 's-Gravenvoeren
☎ 04–3811367

10 Activities

Cycling: there are cycle races from early spring to autumn, but it is of course also possible to cross the country by bicycle yourself. For example, in the Flemish Ardennes (➤ 25).

Shopping: Antwerp and Hasselt have a reputation as fashion cities. Brussels is a good place to look for antiques.

Penance procession in Veurne

Watching sand yacht races: regular sand yacht races are held on the wide beach near De Panne (▶ 56) – sometimes at speeds of up to 120kph (75mph)!

Walking: large parts of Flanders are suitable for exploring on foot. In the Kempen (▶ 39) there are nearly 300 signposted paths.

Going on a hot-air balloon trip: during a hot-air balloon trip you have a breathtaking view over the Flemish polders. St Niklaas is a beautiful starting point (▶ 66).

Admiring statues: Flanders is rich in sculpture. In Middelheim Park (▶ 32) you will find one of the most beautiful open-air collections of classical and contemporary sculpture.

Beach volleyball: all along the coast there are plenty of opportunities for playing a game of beach volleyball. Especially in Blankenberge (▶ 48) where volleyball is played with fanatical enthusiasm.

Wagon trip: in Limburg (▶ 83) there are several places where you can hire a wagon with driver.

Playing *boules*: in some places they play *boules* in the park in the summer, so you can take a set of balls and join in.

Bird-watching: nature reserve Het Zwin (▶ 26) is ideal for this in the spring. Take binoculars and wellington boots!

10
Events

- Folkloristic procession and pretzel-throwing (Geraardsbergen): last Sunday in February
- Ball of the Dead Rat (Ostend): first Saturday in March
- Cat procession (Ieper): first Sunday in May (every three years from 2000)
- Hanswijk-procession (Mechelen): Sunday before Ascension Day
- Heilig-Bloedprocessie (Bruges, ▶ 44); Ascension Day

A hot-air balloon trip offers a spectacular view across flat Flanders landscape

- Sinksenfoor (Antwerp): large funfair every year in the six weeks after Whitsun
- Torhot/Werchter pop and rock festival: first Friday, Saturday and Sunday in July
- Ghent Festivals: third week in July
- Flower carpet in the Grand-Place (Brussels): 14, 15 and 16 August; during even years
- Giants' procession (Dendermonde): Thursday after the fourth Sunday in August

5
Best Views

- Kemmelberg, Heuvelland
- Atomium, Brussels (▶ 72)
- Belfort, Bruges (▶ 45)
- Papenkelders, Herenthals
- IJzertoren, Diksmuide (▶ 16)

Flemish Brabant

Flemish Brabant is the heart of the Duchy of Brabant, once one of the superpowers of medieval Europe. The province was formed in 1995 when Brabant was split into a Dutch-speaking part and a French-speaking part.

Flemish Brabant has a rich heritage. The begijnhofs (► 6) of Leuven and Diest are amongst the most beautiful in the country. The monumental cloth halls in towns such as Zoutleeuw are reminiscent of the time when the cloth trade flourished.

Centuries ago, Pieter Breughel situated a number of his paintings in the rural Pajottenland. Further east lies the majestic Zoniënwoud, where the age-old beech trees are reminiscent of the pillars of a cathedral.

The painful split of the Belgian state is perfectly illustrated by the status of Brussels. The Belgian capital, officially bilingual but very French in atmosphere, is completely surrounded by Flemish Brabant, but officially is not part of this Dutch-speaking province.

> *'Even when it is pouring with rain, the shopfronts and pavements are still scrubbed.'*
>
> BAUDELAIRE
> *On Brussels in* Pauvre Belgique

———————•———————

Left: *Gate to the Begijnhof, Diest*

Sights in Brussels
The street names and sights on the Brussels map (► 74) are marked in Dutch, as for the rest of this guide. However, we have also given the French names for the major sights in the text as these may be more familiar to some readers.

Brussels

Flemish and Walloon, sophisticated and common, new architecture and art nouveau: this is a city of contrasts. Historic downtown Brussels could be almost anywhere in Flanders, but uptown Brussels with its wide avenues and symmetrical parks could easily be mistaken for a district of Paris.

Brussels is not a city you'll fall in love with at first sight. Some visitors, however, slowly learn to appreciate the charms of the 'European capital' and come back for the much-praised restaurants, museums and antique shops.

Brussels is officially bilingual – both French and Dutch are used on road and street signs. However the city has an unmistakably French atmosphere. The capital of the country is not, however, part of either the Flanders or Walloon provinces. When Belgium was split, it chose as neutral a compromise as possible: the city is now a metropolitan district in its own right and is, in fact, a state within a state.

What to See in Brussels

ATOMIUM ★

On the north side of Brussels stands the Atomium, an iron molecule enlarged 165 billion times, whose scale and shape in particular speaks to the imagination. Just like the Eiffel Tower, the Atomium was built for a world exhibition, held in 1958. The nine atoms of the iron molecule are represented by the same number of gigantic spheres now threatened, ironically enough, with rust. (► 73, 109).

The Atomium also houses a science museum, the spheres linked by escalators.

✚ 80C2
✉ Eeuwfeestlaan
☎ 02–4748977 or 02–4748904
🕐 Sep–Mar: Mon–Sun 10–6; Apr–Aug: Mon–Sun 9–8
🚇 Heizel
♿ Few
👆 Moderate

The 110m-high Atomium. In the foreground, scale models of Big Ben and the Houses of Parliament

CENTRE BELGE DE LA BANDE DESSINÉE
(CENTRUM VAN HET BEELDVERHAAL) ✪✪✪

The Centre Belge de la Bande Dessinée, commonly referred to as the 'Stripmuseum', is one of Brussels' top attractions. This comic-strip museum is housed in the former Waucquez stores, a creation by art nouveau architect, Victor Horta. The collection contains not only a large number of original drawings, but also three-dimensional models, such as the famous Tintin rocket.

GRAND-PLACE (GROTE MARKT ► 17, TOP TEN) ✪✪✪

🏠 74B4
✉ Zandstraat
☎ 02–2191980
🕐 Tue–Sun 10–6. Closed on 1 Jan, Easter and 25 Dec
🍴 Pub-restaurant Horta on the ground floor (£)
🚇 Centraal Station or De Brouckere
♿ Moderate

Antique market in the Place du Grand Sablon

PLACE DU GRAND SABLON (GROTE ZAVEL) ✪

This square reflects the stately character of the city. The name refers to the marshy sand plain which was once on this site. Now a fairly aristocratic neighbourhood stands here, known for its antique shops. At the far end of the square stands the Notre Dame du Sablon (Zavelkerk), where an antique market is held every weekend.

Just past the square, in the Egmont public gardens, are statues of the Counts of Egmont and Hoorn. The counts, who together with William of Orange were Alva's main opponents, were beheaded in the Grand-Place in 1568. The aristocracy was most upset: to send someone of your own social class to the scaffold was not the done thing!

🏠 74B2
✉ Grote Zavel
🍴 Various cafés and restaurants in the Grote Zavel, such as café Le Grain de Sable (£) or tearoom Le Pain Quotidien (£–££)
🚇 Naamse Poort
♿ Musées Royaux des Beaux-Arts (► 76)

DID YOU KNOW?

In the year 2000, the Brussels Minister of Finance launched a plan to turn the Atomium into a casino. The income would be used to pay for the restoration of the building.

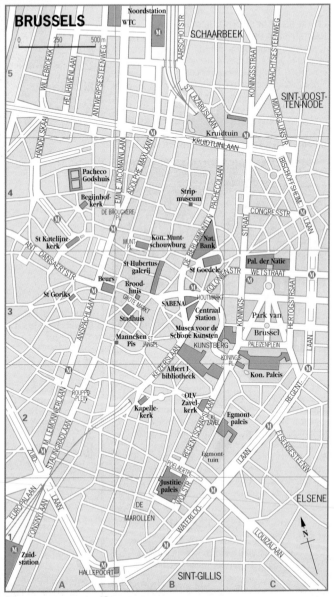

PARC DU CINQUANTENAIRE (JUBELPARK) ✪

Brussels has a large number of parks. This is one of the best-known, located southeast of the city centre. It was created on the occasion of the fiftieth anniversary of Belgium's independence. King Leopold II, who in the Congo had acquired considerable wealth, developed it into a prestigious park, complete with a colossal arc de triomphe. The several museums in the park include one devoted to different world civilisations.

MANNEKEN PIS ✪

Manneken Pis is the city's most notorious inhabitant. This statue may be disappointingly small and is sited fairly far back, but you have to see (and photograph) it

once. There are several stories about the origins of the Manneken Pis statue. According to one, a wealthy resident of Brussels had lost his young son at a party in the Grand-Place. When he found him – peeing and safe – he was so moved that he commissioned a sculptor to preserve the scene forever. Another story is that the little man had once extinguished the fuse of a bomb intended for the Grand-Place. Manneken Pis now has a sister statue called Jeanneken Pis.

🔢 80C2
✉ Jubelpark 10
☎ 02–7417211
🕐 Tue–Sun 9:30–5. Closed 1 Jan, 1 May, 1 Nov, 11 Nov and 25 Dec
🚇 Merode, Schumann
💶 Moderate
♿ Good (wheelchairs available)

🔢 74B3
✉ Manneken Pis: Stoofstraat; Jeanneken Pis: Getrouwheidsgang (a side street off the Beenhouwersstraat)
🍴 Poechellenkelder (£) in the Eikstraat and numerous café-restaurants in and around the Grand-Place
🚇 Beurs
↔ Grand-Place (► 17)

Above: *Parc du Cinquantenaire*

The small but world-famous Manneken Pis

🚩 74B1

✉ Blaesstraat, Hoogstraat, Vossenplein

🍴 Various brasseries and cafés in the Blaesstraat and the Hoogstraat, such as Indigo (£); Stekerlapatte in the Priestersstraat (£–££)

🚩 74B3

✉ Regentschapsstraat 3

☎ 02–5083211

🕐 Tue–Sun 10–5. Closed on 1 Jan, 1 May, 1 Nov, 11 Nov, 25 Nov and on the second Thursday of Jan

Ⓔ Centraal Station

⚐ Moderate

↔ Place du Grand Sablon (► 73)

Above: the first covered street in Europe: the St Hubert shopping arcade

MAROLLES (MAROLLEN)

The Marolles has traditionally been a working-class district but over the years the antique dealers have moved in. Lovers of old utensils can rummage to their heart's content in the second-hand junk shops. In the Place du Jeu de Belle (Vossenplein), the heart of the neighbourhood, a daily flea market is held. The Marolles is also known for its gables decorated with figures from comic strips, which give this neighbourhood a colourful appearance.

MUSÉES ROYAUX DES BEAUX-ARTS (KONINKLIJKE MUSEA VOOR DE SCHONE KUNSTEN) ✪✪

Extending for some distance along the Rue de la Régence (Regentschapsstraat) to the west of the Palais de Justice (Paleis van Justitie), this is actually a double museum as one section is devoted to old Masters and the other to modern art. In the museum of older art hangs the work of well-known masters such as Rubens, van Dyck, Jacob Jordaens, Frans Hals and Jan Steen. The museum of modern art represents the most important movements of the 20th century. In addition to Belgian artists such as Magritte, Delvaux and Ensor, the museum also devotes space to Max Ernst, Miró, Picasso and the painters in the Cobra group.

GALERIES ST HUBERT (ST HUBERTUSGALERIJ) ✪✪

The Galeries St Hubert was the first covered shopping street in Europe. This arcade is popular with street musicians because of its excellent acoustics. It houses chic boutiques, restaurants and cafés, such as the famous Mokafé, where the same old ladies enjoy their pastries day in and day out. The arcade crosses the rue des Bouchers (Beenhouwersstraat), which has more restaurants than any other street in Brussels. The stunning displays of seafood and ice give it the appearance of one long shop-window.

CATHÉDRALE DE ST MICHEL (ST MICHIELSKATHEDRAAL) ✪✪

This mighty cathedral, with two massive main towers, an unusual feature for a church in Belgium stands high on a hill in Brussels. The church was built between the 13th and 15th centuries, and has a number of magnificent stained-glass windows. It also contains the tombs of the Archduke Albrecht and Archduchess Isabella. Equally worthwhile is the baroque pulpit from 1699, with exuberant woodcarvings by the Antwerp sculptor Hendrik Verbruggen. 'A creation in itself,' Victor Hugo wrote of this.

✚ 74B3
✉ St Hubertusgalerij; entrance in the Grasmarkt
🍴 Mokafé (£) and 'Koe die naar de voorbijgaande treinen kijkt' (£) in the arcade; many restaurants in Beenhouwersstraat, such as Aux Armes des Bruxelles (£££)
↔ Grand-Place (► 17)

✚ 74B3
✉ St Goedelevoorplein
☎ 02–2178345
🕐 Mon–Sun 8–6
🚉 Centraal Station
♿ Few, but wheelchairs available on request
💶 Free; entrance fee payable only for the crypt

Cathédrale de St Michel

A Walk Through Brussels

Distance
3.5km (2 miles)

Time
3 hours (with a break)

Start/end point
Grand-Place (Grote Markt)
➕ 74B3

Lunch
Le Pain Quotidien (£–££)
✉ Zavelstraat 11
☎ 02-5135154

This walk, which starts at the Grand-Place (Grote Markt), leads through both downtown and uptown Brussels.

From the Grand-Place, turn into Charles Bulsstraat, the left next to the Hôtel de Ville (Stadhuis).

Don't forget to brush past the copper statue of Everard 't Serclaes, as this is supposed to bring you luck.

Follow the Stoofstraat, a continuation of Charles Bulsstraat, up to the corner with the Eikstraat.

This is the location of the most famous statue in Belgium: Manneken Pis (▶ 75). The small fountain has been here since 1619 and was made by Hiëronymus Duquesnoy.

Turn left into the Eikstraat up to the Oudkorenhuisplein, then turn right into the Dinantstraat. Cross the Keizerslaan via the Dinantplein. Via the Rollebeekstraat you will reach the Place du Grand Sablon (Grote Zavel).

The smart-looking Place du Grand Sablon (▶ 73) is dominated by the church. On Saturdays there is an antique market.

Musées Royaux des Beaux-Arts

Go straight on into the Zavelstraat and, at the end, turn left into the Regentschapstraat.

On your left, you will see the museums for old and modern art, which together form the Musées Royaux des Beaux-Arts (Koninklijke Musea voor de Schone Kunsten, ▶ 76).

At the Koningsplaats, opposite the equestrian statue of Godfried van Bouillon, turn left into the Hofbergstraat. Via the steps of the Kunstberg you come to the Albertinaplein. Turn (diagonally) right into the Magdalena Steenweg, which comes out onto the Grasmarkt. Return to the Grand-Place via the Koninginnegalerij (right turn), the Beenhouwersstraat (left turn) and the Korte Beenhouwersstraat (left turn).

Opposite: Fonske is a symbol of student life in Leuven

What to See in Flemish Brabant

LEUVEN (LOUVAIN) ●●●

Leuven is especially known for its university, which was founded in 1425. Its students have included the cartographer Mercator and Emperor Charles V. Famous scholars such as Lipsius and Erasmus taught here. Leuven still has a high concentration of students: more than a quarter of the population is registered with one of the faculties. Student life centres on the cafés of the Oude Markt.

The city centre of Leuven is rich in statues that are not only found in the numerous alcoves of the Gothic Town Hall, but also grace the public gardens, squares and street corners. The most well-known one is **Fonske**. This statue by Jef Claerhout represents the stereotypes of student life: Fonske pours equal quantities of knowledge and beer into his hollow skull. Fonske is a corruption of the official Latin name, *Fons Sapientiae*, or 'source of wisdom'.

The Leuven **Groot Begijnhof** is the largest almshouse complex in the country. This begijnhof (➤ 6) was founded at the beginning of the 13th century. In the following centuries, life at the begijnhof became so popular that it grew into a 'city within a city', complete with bridges, a village pump, gardens and its own church. Most of the brick houses and convents date from the 17th and 18th centuries. Where unmarried women once carried out their devout labour, now hangs the smell of *waterzooi* and chilli con carne: these days, the begijnhof is inhabited by students and staff from Leuven University, as is obvious from the many nameplates by the door.

Other sights include St Pieterskerk, a late Gothic building with a dramatic baroque pulpit.

STADHUIS (➤ 24, TOP TEN)

➕ 81D2

Fonske
✉ Fochplein
🍴 Various café-restaurants in the Grote Markt, such as Gambrinus (£) and Klein Tafelrond (£)
↔ Stadhuis (➤ 23) and St Pieterskerk

Groot Begijnhof
✉ The begijnhof is located between Redingenstraat, Zwarte Zustersstraat and Schapenstraat. The main entrance is in Schapenstraat
🕐 Begijnhof church: Apr–Sep:Tue–Sun 1–4
🚌 Naamse Poort bus 2

✚ 81F3
✉ Begijnenstraat
🕐 Begijnhof: daily;
St Katharinakerk:
Easter–Oct: Sun 2–5

DIEST BEGIJNHOF   ✪✪

As is the case with Leuven's Groot Begijnhof, Diest
Begijnhof has been beautifully preserved. The begijnhof
(►6) was founded in 1253. The baroque entrance gate
carries the words, *Comt in mynen Hof, myn suster Bruyt*, a
verse from the *Song of Songs*. Although most houses and
convents in the complex are now used as workshops, this
begijnhof has retained its secluded character.

The 14th-century St Katharinakerk, in the middle of the
complex, is especially known for its rococo interior and its
elaborate pulpit.

✚ 80A–80B
Kasteel van Gaasbeek
✉ Kasteelstraat
☎ 02–5310130
🕐 Apr–Oct: daily 10–5.
Closed Mon (except
Jul–Aug) and Fri
👖 Moderate
♿ Few

PAJOTTENLAND   ✪

The landscape of Pajottenland is characterised by gently
rolling fields and meadows, as well as rows of poplars and
pollarded willows. The main attraction in this area is **Kasteel
van Gaasbeek**. The Count of Egmont spent his last days in
this castle, before being beheaded in Brussels.

The castle now houses a museum, where you will find
displays of wood-carvings and tapestries from Brussels
and Doornik.

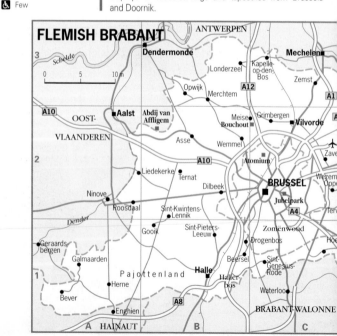

ZONIËNWOUD

Southeast of Brussels lies the stately Zoniënwoud. Initially, this wood served as a hunting ground for dukes and kings. At the end of the 19th century, beech trees were planted here and the dense coverage of leaves ensures that low-growing plants have little chance of establishing themselves. In the summer, the wood has the appearance of an enormous cathedral, where thick tree-trunks rise up like pillars. Near Tervuren in the northeast is the Museum voor Midden-Afrika (Museum of Central Africa).

- 80C1
- Leuvensesteenweg 13
- 02–7695211
- Tue–Fri 10–5, Sat–Sun 10–6. Closed 1 Jan and 25 Nov
- Cheap; extra charge for special exhibitions
- Brussels (➤ 72–8)

ZOUTLEEUW, ST LEONARDUSKERK

In 1566, large parts of Flanders were subjected to iconoclastic fury. As a protest against Spanish occupation, the population destroyed many church interiors. The robbers ignored the town of Zoutleeuw, however, which is why the Gothic St Leonarduskerk is the only church in Belgium whose medieval interior is still intact. It has a wealth of religious art works, such as the fine sacrament tower from 1552: a tabernacle cut from stone and decorated with many scenes from the Bible.

- 81F2
- Grote Markt
- 011–781288
- Easter–Sep: Tue–Sun 2–5; Oct: Sat–Sun 2–5
- Cheap

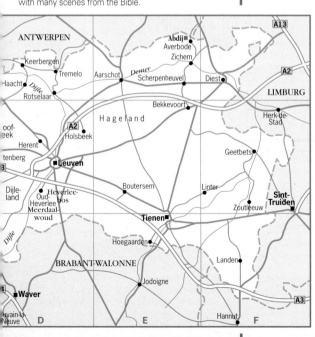

Limburg

Historically, Limburg has been regarded as the Flanders province where industry has had the greatest impact. These days, Limburg is particularly praised for its scenery: the green valleys of the Voerstreek (► 89), the area of Maasland so rich in water, and the extensive forests of the Limburgse Kempen which draw many nature lovers every year. The province is at its most beautiful in spring, when the fruit trees of the Haspengouw (► 18) are blossoming.

Limburg has a special position within the Flemish region. The inhabitants of the province often feel more closely related to their Dutch 'neighbours' than to their fellow countrymen, who sometimes have difficulty in understanding their Limburg dialect. The heart of the province, Hasselt, is known for gin production and for its fashion. A little further south lies Tongeren, the oldest city in Belgium, once feared by Julius Caesar.

> *'Of all these, the Belgians are the bravest because they are the furthest removed from civilisation.'*
>
> JULIUS CAESAR

———•———

Left: *a beautiful lake in the vicinity of Altembrouck Castle (Voerstreek)*

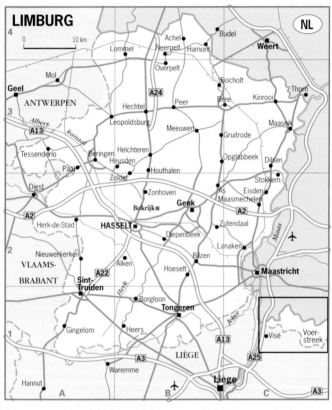

LIMBURG

NL

0   10 km

Achel   Budel

Neerpelt   Hamont   **Weert**

Lommel   Overpelt

Mol   Bocholt   Thorn

Geel   Hechtel   Peer   Bree   Kinrooi

ANTWERPEN   A24

Albert-   Leopoldsburg   Maaseik

A13   kanaal   Meeuwen

Tessenderlo   Helchteren   Gruitrode

Beringen   Opglabbeek   Dilsen

Paal   Heusden   Houthalen   Stokkem

Zolder   Eisden

Diest   Zonhoven   As   Maasmechelen

A2   Bokrijk   **Genk**   A2

Herk-de-Stad   **HASSELT**   Zutendaal

Diepenbeek   Lanaken

Nieuwerkerken   Bilzen   **Maastricht**

VLAAMS-   Alken

BRABANT   A22   Hoeselt

Sint-Truiden

Herk   Borgloon   **Tongeren**

Ieker

Gingelom   Heers   A13   Visé   Voer-streek

LIÈGE   A25

Hannut   A3

Waremme   **Liège**

A   B   C   A3

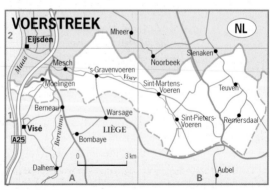

VOERSTREEK

NL

Eijsden   Mheer

Maas   Slenaken

Mesch   Noorbeek

's-Gravenvoeren   Voer   Sint-Martens-Voeren   Teuven

Moelingen

Berneau   Warsage   Sint-Pieters-Voeren   Remersdaal

Visé   LIÈGE

A25   Bombaye

Berwinne   0   3 km

Dalhem   Aubel

A   B

Hasselt

The capital of Limburg, Hasselt, came into being around the 7th century. This third largest trading centre in Flanders is especially known for its gin production. On sunny days, the waiters in the Grote Markt are kept busy serving small glasses of this 'living water'. In addition to gin festivals (▶ 99), there are daily drinks tours and there is even a gin tram.

Hasselt also has a reputation as a city of fashion. The Stedelijk Modemuseum holds regular exhibitions centred on developments in the area of couture. The many exclusive fashion boutiques alternate with historic buildings, such as the Abdij (abbey) and the Refugiehuis van Herkenrode, the St Quintinuskathedraal and the Onze-Lieve-Vrouwebasiliek. There are several new sports facilities and a large cultural centre in the town.

What to See in Hasselt

✚ 84B2

JENEVERMUSEUM ✪

The Nationaal Jenevermuseum is housed in a 19th-century distillery. This museum not only shows the different stages of Dutch gin production, but also highlights the history and folklore surrounding this national drink. In the bar by the museum, visitors can taste what is so unique about the speciality gin of the region: Hasselts Witteke.

✉ Witte Nonnenstraat 19
☎ 011–241144
🕐 Tue–Sun 10–5, Nov–Mar: Sat–Sun 1–5
♿ Moderate

Campers in Limburg

✉ Gasthuisstraat 11
☎ 011–239621
🕐 Tue–Fri 10–5, Sat–Sun
1–5; Apr–Oct: Tue–Sun
and holidays 10–5.
Closed 1–2 Jan, 11 Nov
and 25–26 and 31 Dec
♿ Good
👜 Moderate

*Above: the Modemuseum
highlights both the history
and new trends of fashion*

✚ 84B2
✉ Kasteelstraat 6
☎ 089–519344
🕐 Castle and classic
gardens accessible
during special exhibitions;
group visits on request
👜 Visit to church and
English landscaped park
free
↔ Tongeren (▶ 89)

STEDELIJK MODEMUSEUM ✪

In the Stedelijk Modemuseum (fashion museum), housed
in a former 17th-century convent, you can follow various
developments of fashion from the 18th to the 21st
centuries. Both accessories and clothing from Victorian to
retro and from lace to PVC are on display. Special
exhibitions, such as 'Barbie and Haute Couture', highlight
different aspects of the fashion industry, including mass
culture, lifestyle and the protective function of clothes. The
collection also features fashion photography.

What to See in Limburg Province

ALDEN BIESEN ESTATE, BILZEN ✪✪

Apart from its historic market square, the town of Bilzen is
especially known for the Alden Biesen castle and estate.
The moated castle was once a refuge for members of the
Order of the Teutonic Knights, founded at the time of the
crusades to nurse the sick and wounded in the Holy Land.
The original castle dated from 1220 but, from the 16th
century onwards, it was gradually extended into a luxury
country mansion, with citadels, an orangery and a
beautiful garden.

In order to give blind and partially-sighted people an
impression of the building, one of the castle halls houses
a model of the complex. The historical texts have also all
been translated into Braille.

Interior of De Blauwe Leeuw pharmacy in Maaseik

HASPENGOUW (▶ 18, TOP TEN)

MAASEIK ✪

Maaseik is known as the birthplace of the van Eyck brothers, Jan and Hubert, jointly responsible for *The Adoration of the Mystic Lamb* triptych (▶ 23). The 17th-century monastery of the Minderbroeders has copies of it, as well as an X-ray photograph of the central panel. The town is also home to the oldest private pharmacy in Belgium, *De Blauwe Leeuw* (The Blue Lion). The pestles and mortars, small wooden drawers and tin pots give you the impression that you could just step inside to order a portion of saltpetre. The pharmacy is part of the Museactron, an original three-part hands-on museum.

➕ 84C3
✉ Lekkerstraat 5
☎ 089–566890
🕐 Oct–Mar: Tue–Sun 10–12 and 2–5; Apr–Sep: Tue–Sun 10–5; Jul–Aug: also on Mon
✋ Moderate

Statue of the van Eyck brothers

📍 Not on the map
✉️ Avergat z/n
☎️ 012–455355
🔄 Guided tours with Dutch
   or French-speaking guide
   take place daily at 3.30;
   please reserve
✋ Moderate

St Truiden Town Hall

MERGELGROTTEN VAN KANNE, RIEMST

If you wish to explore the Kanne marlstone caves without a guide, it would be wise to take a ball of red wool with you. In this 300km-maze of caves you would be almost guaranteed to lose your way. The underground vaults were created when marlstone blocks were cut away for the building of churches and fortresses in the Middle Ages.

The wall paintings of prehistoric animals inside the caves give visitors the impression that they have gone thousands of years back in time. The paintings can be appreciated even if you do not understand the Dutch- or French-speaking guide. Part of the cave is now used to cultivate mushrooms, which thrive in the underground micro-climate.

📍 84A1
Trudo-abdij
✉️ Grote Markt
☎️ 011–701818
🔄 Visitor centre of former
   abbey open: Apr–Oct:
   Mon–Sun 9–6; Nov–Mar:
   Mon–Fri 9–4 and Sat 9–6
🍴 Theatre (£–££) Grote
   Markt 🎫 Free

ST TRUIDEN

The 1300-year-old town of St Truiden is the centre of the Haspengouw fruit-growing region (► 18). St Truiden was built around the **Trudo-abdij**. This abbey was founded by the nobleman Trudo, who was later declared a saint. A statue above the abbey gate shows Trudo healing a blind woman.

The site of the former abbey square is now the Grote Markt, the second largest market square in Belgium. The 18th-century Town Hall, situated in the square, was built around its medieval tower, with a gable made of brick.

TONGEREN ✪✪

Tongeren is the oldest town in Belgium. Tribes settled here as early as the first century BC, including Ambiorix, leader of the Eburones, a fighter who seems to have walked straight out of an Asterix comic book. Under his leadership Belgium managed to withstand the attacks of Julius Caesar for five years, which caused the Emperor to comment that of all the Celts, the *Belgae* were the bravest. The statue of Ambiorix, which has a prominent place in the market square, dates from 1866.

Gallo-Romeins Museum stands on the site of a luxurious Roman villa. Archaeologists are still making new discoveries in the area. The museum gives an overview of prehistoric times up to the Merovingian period.

Statue of Ambiorix in Tongeren

🔲 84B1
Gallo-Romeins Museum
✉ Kielenstraat 15
☎ 012–233914
🕐 Mon–Fri 9–5, Sat–Sun and holidays 10–6. Closed Mon morning
🍴 De Brasserie (££), Grote Markt or Het Kanunnikenhof (£££), Vermeulenstraat
✋ Moderate
↔ Haspengouw (▶ 18), Alden Biesen (▶ 86)

VOERSTREEK ✪✪✪

The Voerstreek has a curious status, the enclave of six villages is surrounded by a French-speaking area. This situation has long been a thorn in the side of some of the population, who plead for inclusion in the Walloon provinces. The former mayor of the municipality, José Happart, became notorious in the early 1990s because of his refusal to speak Dutch at public events. The region, which is crossed by the Voer River, is characterised by hawthorn hedges and timber-framed houses in silex stone. The landscape is green, luscious and varied. The highest point in Flanders (287.5m) is found on the ridge of one of the slopes, in St Martens-Voeren.

🔲 84C1
🍴 Herberg Moeder de Gans in Teuven (££) or Herberg De Swaen in 's-Gravenvoeren (££)
🚌 From NMBS station Visé, two buses go to the Voerstreek: 39C and 39B

DID YOU KNOW?

St Martens-Voeren is dominated by a 23m-high railway bridge. This bridge was built during World War I by order of the Germans. Two thousand Russian prisoners of war were involved in the building process.

A Drive Through South Limburg

Distance
150km (93 miles)

Time
6 hours

Start/end point
Hasselt
➕ 84B2

Lunch
Moeder de Gans (££)
✉ Dorpsstraat 6, Teuven
☎ 04–3812285

The Altembroek estate in the Voerstreek

This tour departs from Hasselt (➤ 85).

Take the N20 in the direction of Tongeren. After 4km (2.5 miles) turn right at Wimmertingen to Alken, then take the N759 (left turning) in the direction of St Truiden. At Ordingen, take the N79 to St Truiden.

The noteworthy features of St Truiden (➤ 88) are the Town Hall and the imposing St Trudo Abbey.

Take the N3 in the direction of Luik. After 10km (6 miles) turn left on to the N784 at Heers in the direction of Borgloon.

Borgloon is the heart of the Haspengouw (➤ 18), Belgium's fruit-growing region. The place is surrounded by castles.

Continue the route via the N76 to Hasselt (➤ 85) and Genk. After 3km (2 miles) turn right at Kerniel, in the direction of Gors-Opleeuw. Via Schalkhoven you reach Hoeselt, where you continue in the direction of Kleine Spouwen and Riemst.

A few kilometres past Hoeselt lies the former estate of Alden Biesen (➤ 86), the largest castle complex in Flanders.

At Kleine Spouwen, take the N745 to Riemst (➤ 88). The road changes into the N671 to Zichen-Zussen-Bolder and Eben, where you go down to Visé via the N671.

Now cross a small strip of the Walloon province to reach the Voerstreek (➤ 89), a Dutch-speaking enclave in a French-speaking area.

At Visé, head towards Moelingen. Drive on in an easterly direction to Teuven via 's-Gravenvoeren, St Martens-Voeren and St Pietersvoeren.

Teuven is a picturesque town with timber-framed cottages, two castles and a number of restaurants. Surrounded by undulating landscape with extensive woods, Teuven is ideally placed for exploration on foot.

Drive the same way back to Visé. Then take the N618 to Tongeren and follow the N20 to Hasselt.

Where to...

Above: *part of the Flemish coast changes into one long terrace in the summer*
Right: *Kwak beer has its own character and its own glass*

Antwerp

Prices
Prices are approximate, based on a three-course meal for one, without drinks or service:
£ = less than 20 euros (BF800)
££ = 20–40 euros (BF800–1600)
£££ = more than 40 euros (BF1,600)

Opening Times
Most restaurants in Flanders are open from midday until midnight. Between 3PM and 6PM, many restaurants are closed.

Dock's Café (££)
Dock's Café is known not only for its baroque interior by the Portuguese architect Antoine Pinto, but also for the fantastic oyster bar on the first floor. The restaurant is slightly reminiscent of a cruise ship; guests look out on the River Scheldt from behind a copper railing.
The fish cuisine has been a concept amongst the Antwerp beau monde for years. The prawn croquettes seem to be the best in town and the wine list is a delight if somewhat pricey. Lunch and dinner.
⊠ Jordaenskaai 7
☎ 03–2266330
🕔 Closed Sat afternoon
🚌 Bus 6, 34

Het Elfde Gebod (£)
For years now, the Elfde Gebod has been proof that the church and the pub can happily co-exist. Guests are surrounded by a collection of saints' statues which would make any place of worship envious. The terrace covered in ivy at the foot of the Onze-Lieve-Vrouwe-kathedraal is, especially in the summer months, an attractive venue.
⊠ Torfbrug 10, Antwerp
☎ 03–2323611
🚌 2, 3, 4, 7, 8, 10, 11, 15

Den Engel (£)
Den Engel is a typical Antwerp café where nothing ever seems to change. Popular with a variety of customers during the week and frequented especially by Dutch visitors at the weekend.
⊠ Grote Markt 3
☎ 03–2331252
🚌 2, 3, 4, 7, 8, 10, 11, 15

De Foyer (£–££)
Impressive and atmospheric brasserie on the first floor of the Bourlaschouwburg (theatre). Lunch and dinner served.
⊠ Komedieplaats 18 (Bourlaschouwburg), Antwerp
☎ 03–2335517 🚌 7, 8, 12, 24; bus 1, 9, 23

Hippodroom (££)
The sparse interior of the Hippodroom is situated at the back of an art-deco former cinema. The name of the restaurant is a reminder of the time when there was a racecourse here. The refined French cuisine draws many visitors, particularly in the evening. Try the cod with mustard. Lunch and dinner.
⊠ Leopold de Waelplaats 10
☎ 03–2388936
🕔 Closed Sat afternoon and Sun
🚌 Leopold de Waelplaats, 8

Hollywood Witloof (££)
One of the most remarkable restaurants in Antwerp is Hollywood Witloof. Guests eat in a cellar vault which looks more like a submarine, in the light of lamps made from old Perrier bottles. The name of this rather exquisite restaurant was taken from Patrick Conrad's book *Hollywood With Love*. A real must.
⊠ Hofstraat 9 ☎ 03–2337331
🚌 Groenplaats 2, 3, 4, 8, 15

Karbonkel Café (£)
The playful interior and surprisingly spacious Karbonkel Café draws a fashionable and young public, especially in the evening.
⊠ Groenplaats 33, Antwerp
☎ 03–2331045
🚌 Groenplaats 2, 3, 4, 8, 15

De Muze (£)

De Muze is one of the most beautiful cafés in Antwerp and is a great meeting-place for lovers of jazz, which is played live here. The café has three floors, but customers can see the stage, which is on the ground floor, from almost anywhere.

🖂 Melkmarkt 15, Antwerp
☎ 03–2260126
🚊 Groenplaats 2, 3, 4, 8, 15

Pasta (£–££)

This restaurant manages to fill its three floors every night, due to its delicious pasta. The combination of affordable and tasty Italian cuisine and Roman frescoes is very popular with many tourists. The top floor offers a beautiful view across the city. Lunch and dinner.

🖂 Oude Koornmarkt 32
☎ 03–2331776
🕔 Closed Sat and Sun afternoon
🚊 Groenplaats 2, 3, 4, 8, 15

Rooden Hoed (££)

The open fire looks real and the view of the Onze-Lieve-Vrouwekathedraal is splendid. Classic menus served in stylish surroundings. Lunch and dinner.

🖂 Oude Koornmarkt 25
☎ 03–2332844
🚊 Groenplaats 2, 3, 4, 8, 15

Sir Anthony van Dijck (£££)

Chef-owner Marc Paesbrugghe handed back his two Michelin stars in order to be rid of the pressure to perform, which does not detract from the fact that the quality of his French-orientated cuisine remains as good as ever. Lunch and dinner.

🖂 Vlaykensgang, Oude Koornmarkt 16, Antwerp
☎ 03–2316170
🕔 Closed Sat–Sun
🚊 Groenplaats 2, 3, 4, 8, 15

Zuiderterras (££)

The magnificent location alone, at the end of the walkway along the River Scheldt, justifies a visit to the Zuiderterras, a creation of Antwerp's star architect van Reeth. The light, fresh cuisine is also worthwhile. You need to reserve a table here. Lunch and dinner.

🖂 Ernest van Dijckkaai 37
☎ 03–2341275
🚌 Bus 6, 34

Bistro Botanica (£–££)

In this cosy bistro you can have a good and inexpensive meal. In the heart of the city centre.

🖂 Leopoldstraat 24
☎ 032251004
🕔 Mon–Sun 11:30–10, Fri–Sat to midnight

Studio Bazaar (£–££)

In the afternoon it is bistro time with pasta or a lunch menu for around 7 euros (BF300). In the evening you can have a wonderful dinner in this restaurant and enjoy a seven-course menu, including delicious dishes of eel and fresh game.

🖂 Waalsekaai 54
☎ 032169701
🕔 Mon–Thu 11:30–3 and 6:30–10, Fri 11:30–10:30, Sat 6:30–10:30

Corsendonk

Corsendonk Priory is known not only for its Gothic cellar vaults and Renaissance park, but also for two types of beer which are brewed at this former monastery complex. Corsendonk Agnus is a full-flavoured lager, while Corsendonk Pater is soft and dark. Both beers taste excellent with a chunk of Corsendonk cheese.

West Flanders

The Bruges Bear
The names of many cafés, shops and restaurants in Bruges refer to a bear. This animal also has an important place in the city's coat of arms. When the first Duke of Flanders, Baudouin with the Iron Arm, arrived at what is now Bruges, the first living creature he encountered was a bear.

Bruges
Chagall (£)
Cosy restaurant with big fireplace and stained-glass windows. Belgian specialities such as *paling in the groen* (eel with herbs), scampi and mussels with ribsteaks. Lunch and dinner.
⊠ St Amandsstraat 40
☎ 050–336112 🖃 all

Het Dagelijks Brood (£)
Het Dagelijks Brood not only sells fresh bread and cakes, but you can also eat here at a long wooden table. The menu includes salads, sandwiches and extensive Tuscan lunches.
⊠ Philipstockstraat 21
☎ 050–336050 ⓒ Closed Tue

La Dentellière (££)
This restaurant, close to the Minnewater, is especially well known for its regional dishes and steaks.
⊠ Wijngaardstraat 33
☎ 050–331898 ⓒ Closed Tue.

't Dreupelhuisje (£)
More than a hundred different types of gin in somewhat dim surroundings.
⊠ Kemelstraat 9
ⓒ Closed Tue.

Gran Kaffee de Passage (£)
At a reasonable distance from the city centre is the Gran Kaffee de Passage, an elongated pub serving food at small tables. Pleasant atmosphere. Although the menu is modest and prices are low, the cuisine is excellent.
⊠ Dweersstraat 26
☎ 050–340234 🖃 dinner

't Koffieboontje (£)
't Koffieboontje is part of a small hotel with the same name. This pub serves a great variety of snacks, Flemish specialities and vegetarian food.
⊠ Hallestraat 4
☎ 050–338027

't Pandreitje (£££)
't Pandreitje is especially known for its excellent fish dishes, such as fish pie with smoked eel. Diners enjoy the comfort of plush seats, which perhaps they deserve considering the steep prices on the menu. Lunch and dinner.
⊠ Pandreitje 6
☎ 050–331190
ⓒ Closed Wed and Sun
🖃 1, 6, 11, 16

Toermalijn (££)
Generally speaking, Flemish cuisine is not geared towards vegetarians and vegetarian restaurants are usually found only in the big cities. One of these is Toermalijn, housed in the Alfa-Dante Hotel. Lunch and dinner.
⊠ Coupure 29A
☎ 050–340194

Knokke-Heist
Les Flots Blues (££)
This atmospheric restaurant on the Zeedijk specialises in fish and shellfish. It has a nice terrace in the summer months. Lunch and dinner.
⊠ Zeedijk-Albertstrand 538
☎ 050–602710 ⓒ Closed Wed

Ostend
Den Artiest (£)
Pub full of cigarette smoke, live music, dark panelling and an art gallery. Good environment for late-night talking over drinks.
⊠ Kapucijnenstraat 13
☎ 059–808889

Ghent

De Acht Zaligheden (££)

Between the Patershol district and the Vrijdagmarkt this is a good place for an extensive Burgundian meal in quiet surroundings. The amount of light makes this an unromantic restaurant. Lunch and dinner.

- Oudburg 4 ☎ 09–2243197
- Closed Mon
- 1, 10, 11, 12, 13

Amadeus (£–££)

A typical Ghent café which seems to have gone out of its way to make the space look as cluttered as possible. Checked table cloths, coloured lamps, a low ceiling and straightforward cuisine with much meat: cosy!

- Plotersgracht
- ☎ 09–2251385 Dinner
- 1, 10, 11, 12, 13

Brasserie Aba-jour (£)

Beautiful long narrow café with smoky interior.

- Oudburg 20
- ☎ 09–2340729
- 1, 10, 11, 12, 13

De Drie Biggetjes (££–£££)

De Drie Biggetjes restaurant is in one of the most atmospheric streets in Patershol. Less informal than most other restaurants in the area, and the classic French cuisine aims at a slightly wealthier public.

- Zeugsteeg 7 ☎ 09–2242648
- 1, 10, 11, 12, 13

Faits Divers (££)

The idiosyncratic cuisine of Faits Divers in the heart of Ghent is a breath of fresh air amongst the many average restaurants in this area. Unfortunately, the waiting times can be quite long when it is busy. Lunch and dinner.

- Korenmarkt 31 ☎ 09–2330601
- 1, 10, 11, 12, 13

La Malcontenta (££)

Tapas and specialities from the Canary Islands.

- Haringsteeg 9
- ☎ 09–2241801
- 1, 10, 11, 12, 13

De Onvrije Schipper (£)

This modest café is in one of the finest buildings on the Korenlei. You can chat and read over your coffee during the winter months and in the summer it has one of the city's most beautiful terraces.

- Korenlei 7a
- ☎ 09–2336045 Snacks
- 1, 10, 11, 12, 13

Vier Tafels (££–£££)

The most truly international restaurant in Ghent, if not in the whole of Belgium. The dishes on the menu are best described by the term 'fusion', a mixture of cooking styles from all corners of the earth: from Ghent *waterzooi* to reindeer carpaccio, and from crocodile steaks to sushi. A culinary adventure! Lunch and dinner.

- Plotersgracht 6
- ☎ 09–2250525
- 1, 10, 11, 12, 13

Wijnrestaurant Othello (££)

As the name indicates, this restaurant has developed its dishes around its customers' choice of wines, from its very extensive wine list. In summer, you can eat outside in the small courtyard.

- Ketelvest 8
- ☎ 09–2330009
- 1, 10, 11, 12, 13

Moeder Siska

During a visit to Knokke you will sooner or later be offered Moeder Siska's (Mother Siska's) waffles. The fame of these waffles dates back to 1892 when Mother Siska started her waffle stall. The recipe, which has been passed on from generation to generation, is a closely guarded secret.

Brussels

Burgundian Lifestyle

Many foreigners are surprised by the fact that the Flemish enjoy a small drink in a café at any time of day – however early. This phenomenon is not so much an expression of a wide-spread alcohol problem, but more of a Burgundian lifestyle, which combines the useful – getting up early – with the enjoyable.

Cappuccino

Although many restaurants and cafés in Flanders have cappuccino on the menu, the real Italian version – with steamed milk – is available in few places. Many Flemish restaurants simply put a generous dollop of whipped sweetened cream in their coffee. Only espresso bars in bigger cities serve a genuine cappuccino.

Aux Armes des Bruxelles (££–£££)

This renowned establishment is in the culinary heart of the city, amongst the many restaurants in the rue des Bouchers (Beenhouwers-straat). It is divided into two areas; a bistro with wooden benches, and a more upmarket restaurant obviously aimed at a smarter clientele. You can eat well in either.

✉ **Beenhouwersstraat 13**
☎ 02–5115500
🚇 **Beurs, Centraal Station**
🚋 23, 52, 55, 56, 81; bus 29, 34, 47, 48, 60, 63, 65, 66

Le Cercueil (£–££)

One of the most morbid cafés in the country, but a sight in itself. The themes of Le Cercueil (the coffin) are death and funerals. The tables are made of coffins, the taps spew out 'devil's spit', and the lighting is purple fluorescent strip. For the enthusiast.

✉ **Haringstraat 10–12**
☎ 02–5123077
🚇 **Beurs, Centraal Station**
🚋 23, 52, 55, 56, 81; bus 29, 34, 47, 48, 60, 63, 65, 66

Le Grain du Sable (£)

Simple café where the menus are written in decorative gold letters. Quiet jazz and good coffee.

✉ **Grote Zavel 15/16**
☎ 02–5140583
🚇 **Naamse Poort**

De Koe die naar de voor-bijgaande treinen kijkt (£)

This lunch room has the longest name of any in Brussels and the surrounding area (meaning 'The Cow Who Watches the Trains Go

By'). It serves many different kinds of rolls and an excellent breakfast.

✉ **Koninggalerij 29**
☎ 02–5133336
🚇 **Beurs, Centraal Station**
🚋 23, 52, 55, 56, 81; bus 29, 34, 47, 48, 60, 63, 65, 66

Mokafé (£)

In the middle of the St Hubertusgalerij is the unsurpassed Mokafé, an atmospheric classic in beautiful surroundings. Here you can recuperate from all your efforts and enjoy excellent coffee and cakes, lunch and snacks.

✉ **Koningalerij** ☎ 5117870
🚇 **Beurs, Centraal Station**
🚋 23, 52, 55, 56, 81; bus 29, 34, 47, 48, 60, 63, 65, 66

Le Loup Voyant (£–££)

A variety of cocktails, salads and vegetarian dishes. Meat and fish dishes have been served here for 25 years. You can choose from a wide selection of national and international wines at reasonable prices. The staff is professional and very customer-friendly.

✉ **Avenue De la Couronne**
☎ 02–6400208
🕐 Fri and Sat 9–6

Le Pain Quotidien (£–££)

Luxury bakery-cum-tearoom with many different types of bread, generous salads and delicious truffle cake. In the shop area you can even buy your own cold-pressed olive oil and cider. Breakfast, lunch and tea.

✉ **Grote Zavel 11**
☎ 02–5135154:
Branch also at
✉ **rue Antoine Dansaert 22.**
☎ 02–5022361 🚋 20, 48; bus: 4, 95 🚇 **Naamse Poort**

La Piroque (£–££)

Perfectly hidden at the back of a small alleyway on the Place du Grand Sablon (Grote Zavel) is the exotic eating establishment La Piroque. The menu lists dishes from Senegal, and the smells and tastes immediately transport the diners to a tropical atmosphere.

- ✉ rue St Anne 18
- ☎ 02–5113525
- ◷ Closed Mon
- Ⓠ Naamse Poort

Poesjenellekelder (£)

Small enjoyable café with a view of the famous statue of Manneken Pis. Changing selection of speciality beers and local snacks. The terrace is very busy in the summer.

- ✉ Eikstraat 5 ☎ 02–5119262
- Ⓠ Beurs, Centraal Station
- 🚊 23, 52, 55, 56, 81; bus 29, 34, 47, 48, 60, 63, 65, 66

Resto Bleu de Toi (££)

Tastefully decorated, medieval-looking restaurant which holds regular wine-tasting sessions.

- ✉ Rue des Alexiens 73
- ☎ 02–5024371 Ⓠ Anneessens

Le Roy d'Espagne (£)

Beautifully situated brasserie in a 17th-century guild house, with splendid view over the Grand-Place. Extensive beer list.

- ✉ Grand-Place 1
- ☎ 02–5131127
- Ⓠ Beurs, Centraal Station
- 🚊 23, 52, 55, 56, 81; bus 29, 34, 47, 48, 60, 63, 65, 66

In 't Spinnekopke (££)

In 't Spinnekopke has been very popular with residents of Brussels for years. The restaurant specialises in beer-based stews (such as rabbit in Gueuzebier). The owner is also the author of a cookery book full of recipes using beer.

- ✉ Bloemenhofplein 1
- ☎ 02–5118695
- ✉ Sun–Fri lunch & dinner, Sat only dinner
- Ⓠ St Katelijne or Beurs

Au Stekerlapatte (££)

Lively brasserie hidden in an alleyway close to the Palais de Justice. The traditional Brussels cuisine (with specialities such as *poularde de Bruxelles aux champignons* – Brussels chicken) is especially popular with young people.

- ✉ Priestersstraat 4
- ☎ 02–5128681
- ◷ Closed Mon
- Ⓠ Munthof

De Ultieme Hallucinatie (££)

De Ultieme Hallucinatie is especially known for its splendid art-nouveau interior. At the back is an old-fashioned bar with a wrought-iron counter and stained-glass windows. The wooden benches come from 19th century railway carriages. The restaurant is a little pricey, but there are a number of excellent French and Flemish dishes on the menu. Try the poached fish in Gueuze sauce.

- ✉ Koningsstraat 316
- ☎ 02–2170614 Ⓠ Kruidtuin

La Vieille Halle aux Blés (££)

A classic bistro, just outside the busiest downtown areas. Excellent French cuisine.

- ✉ Place de la Vieille Halle aux Blés 34 ☎ 02–5117326
- Ⓠ Anneessens

Falstaff

Next to the Beurs (Stock Exchange) is one of the most beautiful café-restaurants in Brussels. Falstaff (£–££) has an art-nouveau interior designed by Houbion, a pupil of Horta. The curving lines, mirrors, stained-glass windows and large terrace give the place an almost 19th-century atmosphere. In many other cities, this would push up the price considerably, but with so many competing restaurants that logic fortunately does not apply in Brussels. The dishes are reasonably priced during the day; the predominantly French cuisine is fresh and tasteful. Falstaff is also known for its excellent pastries.

- ✉ Henri Mausstraat 19–25
- ☎ 02–5119877 Ⓠ Beurs
- 🚊 23, 52, 55, 56, 81, 90

Flemish Brabant

D' Artagnan

D'Artagnan (££–£££) is a classic restaurant where the chef regularly prepares speciality dishes such as crocodile and bison. Until recently, there was a café called Het Kraakse on this site, which was extremely popular with students from Leuven. The café, together with the private dwelling next to it, was converted to a restaurant whose interior looks as if it has been there for centuries. The theme of D'Artagnan is, of course, the Three Musketeers. The starter, main course and desert are served as the attack, the conquest and the reconciliation. The reconciliation refers especially to the fate which awaits all guests sooner or later: to have to leave after tasting the delicious house wine.

✉ Krakenstraat 9–11
☎ 016-292626
🕔 Mon–Fri lunch and dinner, Sat only dinner. Closed Sun

Leuven
Carlisse (£)

This enjoyable pub serving food is an airy and cheerfully decorated space with mezzanine floor. It is situated close to the university library.

✉ Arendstraat 1
☎ 016–220101

Den Delper (£)

Usually a quiet pub for a comfortable chat. However the pub is dominated by loud disco music at the weekend.

✉ Parijsstraat 30
☎ 016–201753

Café Gambrinus (£)

This pub is an undisputed classic despite the slow service. There are padded leather seats, marble tables and a wall full of angels in all shapes and sizes. Rolls and snacks are available.

✉ Grote Markt 3
☎ 016–201238
🕔 10AM to midnight

't Klein Tafel Rond (£)

In the morning this is a pleasant place to start the day with a delicious cup of coffee. In the afternoon and evening it is a pub serving food, with a conventional menu.

✉ Grote Markt

De Kleine Zinck (££)

This is a long and narrow restaurant with small tables in long rows. The menu is fairly extensive and has a good number of changing specialities.

✉ Oude Markt 43
☎ 016–291530

Ramberg Hof (£££)

For a smart lunch or dinner, this restaurant in a historic building has an atmospheric courtyard garden and an orangery. Meals can be served outside in summer.

✉ Naamsestraat 60
☎ 016–293272

Universum (££)

Cosy tavern for all ages. The kitchen is open day and night for simple but excellent meals. Universum is the kind of pub and eating establishment where everyone feels at home.

✉ Grote Markt

De Wiering (£)

De Wiering is a romantic pub serving food, with a splendid view of the Dijle. The entrance is unsurpassed and the atmosphere difficult to describe. Hens roam freely in the hall and there is a neglected bar-piano with straw sticking out of it. Goldfish swim in a zinc bathtub. The rural and easy-going, carefree attitude of Flanders is shown at its best in this setting.

✉ Wieringstraat 2
☎ 016–291545
🕔 from 11:30

Le Stuut Resto Crêpe (££)

Come and discover this Breton crêperie northwest of Brussels, in the vicinity of Leuven. You will find an extensive menu, cosy decor and fast service. Sweet and savoury pancakes, quiches and salads are served for lunch or dinner.

✉ Rue Pierre Timmermans 36
☎ 02–4250331
🕔 Mon–Fri 12–2PM and from 6:45PM, Sun 7:30–2PM and 6:45–10PM

Limburg

Hasselt and surroundings

De Beurs (££)
Tasty dishes served in a cosy setting by friendly and helpful staff.

✉ Markt 7, Maaseik
☎ 089–572645
🕐 Tue–Sun 10–2

De Gulden Put (£–££)
This restaurant is also suitable for children, as they serve delicious children's meals as well as the regular menu. There is a pleasant terrace and good access for visitors with disabilities.

✉ Havermarkt 23, Hasselt
☎ 011–220129

Herberg 'De Swaen' (££)
Delicious regional dishes served by friendly staff in an inn dating from 1742. You can have lunch or dinner here.

✉ Kinkenberg 188, 's-Gravenvoeren
☎ 04–3811367

Cap Nord (£–££)
Oyster bar Cap Nord, with its maritime atmosphere, looks out on St Quintinus-kathedraal. Naturally, there is plenty of good seafood on the menu.

✉ Fruitmarkt 26, Hasselt
☎ 011–226585

't Witte Paard restaurant (££)
This restaurant has a large heated terrace where you can sit back and watch the world go by on the Grote Markt. There is also a lovely back garden, where on summer evenings you can eat at beautifully laid tables. You can enjoy home-made ice cream, healthy meals, fast and friendly service, and there is a good, extensive wine list to choose from.

✉ Grote Markt 39, Tienen
☎ 016–820084
🕐 Open all days, except Wed, 9AM to midnight

Tongeren

Biessenhuijs(£££)
On sunny days, you can eat in one of the oldest gardens in Belgium. Here you have the opportunity to choose from summer dishes with delicious beers. The restaurant also serves business lunches, five-course gourmet menus and vegetarian dishes.

✉ Hemelingenstraat 23, Tongeren
☎ 012–234709

De Brasserie (£)
Sophisticated French cuisine with many fish dishes. Light and modern interior.

✉ Grote Markt 31 (hoek Hondsstraat), Tongeren
☎ 012–238551

Kanunnikenhof (£££)
The very atmospheric Kanunnikenhof is in one of the most beautiful places in Tongeren, on the edge of the centre. The restaurant is very suited to an intimate and extended dinner. The courtyard originates from a 13th century monastery behind the Onze-Lieve-Vrouwekerk. On summer days, you can eat in the 18th-century garden.

✉ Vermeulenstraat 3, Tongeren ☎ 012–395172

Restaurant Konings (£££)
Specialises in fish, mussels and game dishes in season.

✉ Oude Fonteinweg 49, Tongeren
☎ 012–237867

Gin
Gin festivals, a gin museum, and a fountain in the shape of a borrelmanneke (small man drinking alcohol): gin plays a very prominent role in Hasselt (► 85). One of the most famous gin establishments is 't Stookerijke, an old pub entirely devoted to the witteke. Those who wish to try out the entire range, need to set aside a week for it. 't Stookerijke has more than 80 kinds of gin in stock.

't Stookerijke (£)
✉ Hemelrijk 80, Hasselt
☎ 011–226348

Antwerp

Prices

Prices for a double room, including breakfast:

£ = under 47 euros (BF1,900)

££ = 47–87 euros (BF1,900–3,500)

£££ = more than 87 euros (BF3,500)

Sleeping on the Water

For a few years now, visitors have been able to stay the night in the Scheldt city in style – on the water. A former Norwegian post ship in the old Antwerp harbour has been converted into the Diamond Princess 'floatel' (££). This luxury cruise ship has 53 cabins and 1 suite. On board are several dance halls, a bar and a restaurant.

✉ St Laureiskaai 2 (Bonapartedok)

☎ 03–2270815

Florida (££)

On the Keyserlei, only a stone's throw from the Centraal Station, stands one of the best, low-budget, hotels in Antwerp.

The rooms are simple but well-appointed, and the breakfast buffet is old-fashionedly abundant.

✉ De Keyserlei 59

☎ 03–2321443

🍴 Diamant

🚋 All trams and buses

Industrie (££)

This unusual hotel stands on the edge of Antwerp's art-nouveau district, Het Zuid, and is a converted mansion. Quiet spacious rooms make this an excellent alternative for those who would rather not drive into the city centre.

✉ Emiel Banningstraat 52

☎ 03–2386600

🚋 8

Granducale (££)

This hotel with a family atmosphere has been established for 28 years. It has comfortable rooms, a cosy breakfast room, and a salon with a terrace to sit outside in the summer. The hotel is 10 minutes' walk from the centre, with bus and tram stops nearby.

✉ St Vincentiusstraat 3

☎ 03–2393724

Café and kamerverhuur 't Katshuis (££)

This is a cosy guesthouse with private entrance. Well-appointed rooms with own shower and toilet. The guesthouse is located only 100m from the Grote Markt in the centre of Antwerp.

✉ Grote Pieter Potstraat 18

☎ 03 2340369

New International Youth Hostel (£–££)

Well-appointed family hotel in the heart of Antwerp. The youth hostel is within walking distance of Centraal Station, the Zoo and plenty of atmospheric pubs, restaurants and other visitor attractions and necessities.

✉ Provinciestraat 256

☎ 03–2300522

Rubenshof (£)

The partly art-nouveau Rubenshof, in the southern Antwerp district, was once the 19th-century house of a cardinal. The hotel now has 24 rooms, all of which have retained their own character, and make a stay at this hotel an unforgettable experience.

✉ Amerikalei 115–117

☎ 03–2370789

🚋 12

Prinse (£££)

Hotel Prinse is situated in one of the most beautiful streets in Antwerp and has a 16th-century courtyard– so if you are not going to stay here, you must at least walk past it. It's not cheap, but this is an extremely comfortable and stylish hotel.

✉ Keizerstraat 63

☎ 03–2264050

🚋 4, 7

Raddison Park Lane Hotel Antwerp (£££)

The Raddison Park Lane is a luxury hotel situated in the heart of the city of Antwerp. The hotel offers its guests the ultimate comfort in one of the 178 rooms and suites. The staff are very friendly and helpful.

✉ Van Eicklei 34

West Flanders and East Flanders

Bruges

Hotel Egmond (£££)
Hotel Egmond welcomes its guests in a quiet country house by the Minne-waterpark. The rooms are atmospheric and have an open fire.
✉ **Minnewater 15**
☎ 050–341445

Ter Duinen (££–£££)
The Ter Duinen hotel is situated on one of the most beautiful canals in Bruges. Rooms with air-conditioning, free parking, and a fantastic breakfast buffet.
✉ **Langerei 52**
☎ 050–330407

't Keizershof (£))
This is a simple but sound hotel, close to the Begijnhof and the Minnewater. Rooms with separate shower on the landing.
✉ **Oostmeers 126**
☎ 050–338728

Gasthof de Gulden Kogge (££)
The Damse Vaart connects Bruges with the picturesque town of Damme and is surrounded by rural polders. By the river, just inside Damme, stands Gasthof de Gulden Kogge, a small hotel with only eight rooms. The adjoining restaurant has an extensive and very reasonable menu.
✉ **Damse Vaart Zuid 12, Damme**
☎ 050–354217

Kortrijk

Belfort (££)
The stylish gable of Hotel Belfort is situated between the Gothic Town Hall and the Halletoren. The rooms are comfortable and have a television and minibar. Restaurant on the premises.
✉ **Grote Markt 53**
☎ 056–222220

Hotel Kyrna (££)
This is a quietly situated hotel in the centre of Kortrijk, just 400m from Centraal Station. There is a cosy cocktail bar. The rooms have a bathroom, television and telephone, and are for two to four people. Breakfast is not included.
✉ **Jan Persijnstraat 20**
☎ 075–214460

Ghent

Adoma (£–££)
Attractive location for both train travellers (Ghent-St Pieter station is around the corner) and drivers – there is ample parking at the front of the property. Unfortunately, the centre of Ghent is rather far away.
✉ **St Denijslaan 19**
☎ 09–2226550

Flandria (£)
Quiet hotel with simple rooms, of which only some have their own shower or bath. Large breakfast.
✉ **Barrestraat 3**
☎ 09–2230626

Hotel Gravensteen (££–£££)
Hotel Gravensteen is housed in a beautiful 19th-century building, looking out on the Gravensteen. It has many up-to-date amenities: a sauna, a sports hall and ample parking. Unfortunately, the standard of the rooms is a little disappointing.
✉ **Jan Breydelstraat 5**
☎ 09–2251150
🚊 **1, 10, 11, 12, 13**

Peak Season in Bruges
Compared to the annual influx of tourists, the number of available hotel beds in Bruges is limited. This means that during the peak season – between the middle of May and the end of September – it can be difficult to find a hotel room, especially at the weekend. If you want to be sure of a room, it is best to reserve one well in advance. Or you could go to one of the towns in the surrounding area, such as Damme, Jabbeke, Ostend or Blankenberge.

Brussels and Flemish Brabant

Flemish Breakfasts
Breakfast is almost always included in the price of a hotel room. Flemish breakfasts are usually generous and vary from a few rolls to a complete breakfast buffet with fresh fruit, cereals, scrambled eggs or fried potatoes. The breakfast buffets at Florida (Antwerp) and Ter Duinen (Bruges) are famous.

Brussels

Art Hotel Siru (££)
Although Hotel Siru, which dates from the 1930s and has been recently renovated, does not make an adventurous impression from the outside, the interior is one big surprise. The hotel rooms are furnished by different Belgian artists. Guests are welcomed in a variety of settings.
- ✉ **Place Rogier 1**
- ☎ **02–2033580**
- Ⓜ **Rogier**

La Légende (£)
Atmospheric old building around a courtyard in the heart of the city. Rooms are plain, but cheap.
- ✉ **Lombardstraat 35**
- ☎ **02–5128290**
- Ⓜ **Bourse**
- 🚌 **23, 52, 55, 56, 81**

Hôtel Bedfort (££–£££)
Four-star hotel at walking distance from Grand-Place in Brussels: 309 rooms. All comforts, minibar, television, telephone, bath and shower. There is a piano-bar, a restaurant and ample parking. It is also possible to rent an apartment for a longer stay.
- ✉ **Rue de Midi 135**
- ☎ **02–5127840**

Hotel Manhattan (££)
Hotel Manhattan is located within walking distance of the Beurs, in a district with an increasing number of night-clubs and strip-bars. The hotel looks out on to a busy main road, so the rooms on the street side can be quite noisy.
- ✉ **Boulevard Adolphe Max 132–140**
- ☎ **02–2191619**

Leuven

Hotel La Royale (£)
This hotel, at a stone's throw from the Central Station, is one of the cheapest in Leuven. The rooms reveal that La Royale has known better times, but after a restoration job, the 'royal' past is giving the rooms a faint glow again.
- ✉ **Martelarenplein 6, Leuven**
- ☎ **016–221252**

Jeff's Guesthouse & Oliveria (££)
Jeff's Guesthouse is a jewel in the heart of Leuven. You won't want to leave once you're here. Good cuisine, and comfortable beds in a friendly mansion where oriental fragrances and colours greet you as soon as the door opens. Six small rooms.
- ✉ **Kortestraat 2, Leuven**
- ☎ **016–238780**

Mechelen

Gulden Anker (££–£££)
The Gulden Anker Best Western hotel and restaurant offers quality comfort in a first-class hotel, situated in the vicinity of the Vrijbroekpark. There are 34 rooms which all exude an atmosphere of peace. The tastefully furnished restaurant serving French and regional dishes will certainly be a worthwhile gastronomic experience.
- ✉ **Brusselssesteenweg 2, Mechelen**
- ☎ **015–422535**

Limburg

Hotel British (££)
The Hotel British is a stylish and hospitable hotel, with friendly staff. The beautiful rooms have all comforts: bathroom, toilet, telephone and television. The hotel is surrounded by a large garden with an attractive terrace. There is a garage for your car and an à la carte restaurant serving good food. The hotel is 1km (half a mile) from Bilzen and 2km (1 mile) from the heart of Alden Biesen.

✉ **Maastrichterstraat 20, Bilzen**
☎ **089–411801**

Bokrijks Gasthof (££)
Bokrijks Gasthof is ideally situated at about 10 minutes drive from the motorway in the Antwerp–Aachen direction, 300m from the Bokrijk domain and 5km (3 miles) from the town of Genk. The hotel serves Belgian dishes, which will certainly taste good after a day's activities.

✉ **Hasseltweg 475, Genk**
☎ **011–229556**

Hotel Atlantis (£££)
Modern, contemporary hotel built up over 30 years, situated in a lovely and quiet wooded area only 2km (1 mile) from the centre of Genk. All 24 rooms have bathroom, toilet, radio, television, trouser-press, minibar and telephone. There is a wonderful sauna as well as a fitness room. The Hotel Atlantis is especially popular with cyclists and walkers, for whom the hotel offers special packages.

✉ **Fletersdel 1, Genk**
☎ **089–356551**

Hostellerie Soete Wey (££)
Very quietly situated hotel in beautiful surroundings, easily accessible via the E313 and the E314. There are 20 comfortable rooms. The Hostellerie Soete Wey offers a breakfast buffet, ample parking, a cosy hotel bar and a good restaurant.

✉ **Kluisstraat 48, Heusden-Zolder**
☎ **011–252066**

Hotel New Carlton (£££)
Hotel New Carlton is a cosy and comfortable four-star hotel on the edge of the city. All rooms have television, telephone and bathroom. Hot evening meals and lunch packs available on request. Family atmosphere.

✉ **Luikersteenweg 232, St Truiden**
☎ **011–672211**

Oeterdal (££)
A pleasant hotel with very comfortable rooms, a good restaurant, and everything necessary to make your stay at this hotel as enjoyable as possible.

✉ **Neeroeterenstraat 41, Opoeteren**
☎ **089–863717**

Haute Couture
Since the breakthrough of 'The Antwerp Six', Antwerp has been considered one of the most important fashion cities in Europe. The leading fashion shops are in the Steenhouwersvest, Kammenstraat and Nationalestraat. At the Lombardenvest (No. 2) is the renowned Louis, which also sells creations by designer Anne Demeulenmeester. The shop of the young designer Anna Heylen is also recommended (No. 44). For haute couture, the area around the Bourlaschouwburg is the best. The most exclusive shops are in the Schutterhofstraat.

Where to Shop in Flanders

Chocolate

The art of chocolate-making is often passed on from one generation to the next. The craft itself involves not only culinary secrets, such as the right proportions of the ingredients, but also strict rules regarding the preservation and consumption of the chocolate itself. The best temperature for storing and eating chocolate is between 15°C and 18°C.

Antwerp

't Appartement

Design and interior design by Philippe Starck and Keith Haring, with a striking collection of brightly coloured clocks.

✉ **Lombardenvest 64**
☎ 03–2272807 🚊 4, 8

La Casa Maya

Mexican utensils, masks and Aztec statues.

✉ **Melkmarkt 21**
☎ 03–2271755 🚊
Groenplaats 2, 3, 4, 8, 15

Het Modepaleis

Fashion designer Dries van Noten was one of 'the Antwerp Six' in 1988, a successful group from the Antwerp fashion academy. His Modepaleis in a 19th-century building has grown into a leading institute of fashion. The formula has been copied in places as far away as Japan.

✉ **Nationalestraat 16**
☎ 03–2339437 🚊 4, 8

Naughty I

Naughty I, one of the trendiest shops in Antwerp, aims at the young public. *The* address for the latest outfits, shiny T-shirts and flared post-hippy trousers.

✉ **Kammenstraat 67**
☎ 03–2133500 🚊 4, 8

Redwood

Wooden art objects and interior decoration.

✉ **Leopoldstraat 33**
☎ 03–2253004 🚊 7, 8

Reinier de Ceuleneer

Beautiful Japanese porcelain and antiques.

✉ **Leopoldstraat 7**
☎ 03–2316324 🚊 7, 8

Stephane Kelian

Tasteful and contemporary collection of hand-made shoes by French designer Stephane Kelian.

✉ **De Keyserlei 3**
☎ 03–2260092
🚇 **Diamant**

Sun Wah Supermarket

The largest supermarket in the Chinese district. Two floors of woks, ready-meals and spices from China, Malaysia and Taiwan.

✉ **Van Wesenbekestraat 16–18**
☎ 03–2260459

Chinatown

The area in Antwerp around the Van Wesenbekestraat, behind the Koningin Astridplein, is known as 'Chinatown'. However it is not really a fully-fledged Chinese neighbourhood since it is limited to a few Chinese and Vietnamese restaurants and a handful of shops selling Asian foodstuffs.

ZNJ

Due to the success of this contemporary and completely Flemish fashion label, the ZNJ shops are beginning to take root in different cities.

✉ **Lombardenvest 56**
☎ 03–2030777
🚊 4, 8

West Flanders

Bruges

Kantjuweeltje

Family firm producing hand-made lace. You will find an extensive collection of handkerchiefs, tablecloths and carpets, both new and antique. Bobbin-lace demonstrations every day at 3 o'clock in the shop.

✉ Philipstockstraat 10–11
☎ 050–334225
🚋 4,8

Van Oost

Delicious, real Belgian praline chocolates are sold here.

✉ Wollestraat 9

Raaklijn

The best bookshop in Bruges has a large selection of local and foreign books, as well as books on art movements.

✉ St Jacobsstraat 7
☎ 050–336720

Woolstreet Company

This small shop not only has 450 kinds of Belgian beer, but also the glasses to go with them. Fun to buy as a present.

✉ Wollestraat 31a
☎ 050–348383
🚋 1,6, 11, 16

Evergem
Pralimar

A first-rate place to buy Belgian chocolates.

✉ Beekstraat 68
☎ 09–2570540

Ghent
Counts Gallery

Pretty souvenirs, miniatures, pictures, greeting cards, school documentation, engravings and art objects, including the watchtower of Ghent in tin or bronze. Very competitive prices.

✉ Rekelingenstraat 1
☎ 09–2253127

Katherine Bouckaert

Ornaments and utensils for interior decoration, including a fine collection of vases.

✉ Walpoortstraat 26
☎ 09–2236193
🚋 5, 50

The Fallen Angel

You can browse for hours in this small shop. Antique toys, old picture postcards and devotional pictures.

✉ Jan Breydelstraat 29
☎ 09–2239415
🚋 1, 10, 11, 12, 13

Movies N.V.

Trendy clothing sold in fashion-conscious shop, where the staff sometimes appear to confuse a 'cool' attitude with indifference.

✉ St Pietersnieuwstraat 5
☎ 09–2235912
🚋 5, 50

Pili-Pili

Beautiful original and rare ethnic and silver jewellery.

✉ Penshuisje 5–6,
Groentenmarkt Ghent
☎ 09–2336771

Ri-Kiki

Trendy shoes, sports shoes and boots with platform heels; this shop is especially popular with young customers.

✉ St Pietersnieuwstraat 82
☎ 09–2233022 🚋 5, 50

Lace

Many Flemish cities owe their wealth to the production of English lace as far back as the 13th century. Hand-made lace is still one of the most popular souvenirs. Unfortunately, the craft of the bobbin lacemaker is slowly dying out. Because of its scarcity, the prices of hand-made lace are steadily rising, so that many shops are forced to import from China.

Antoine Dansaert

The rue Antoine Dansaert is considered to be the hippest street in Brussels. Places to eat and fashion boutiques are constantly mushrooming, so that the previously somewhat staid district southeast of the street is slowly becoming the centre of fashionable Brussels. The fashion shop Stijl has collections of established, as well as, new fashion designers.

✉ rue Antoine Dansaert
☎ 02–5130313
🚌 63, 23, 52, 55, 56, 81

Flemish Brabant and Brussels

Brussels

Ajna

If you're looking for a book on spirituality, this New Age bookshop is your best bet. Extensive collection, ranging from Buddhism and Taoism to astrology and tarot.

✉ **Magdalena Steenweg 27, Brussels**
☎ **02–5129393**
🚇 **Centraal Station**

Antik Blaes

In the middle of the Brussel's antiques district is Antik Blaes, a curious mixture of old shop furniture and bric-à-brac on two floors. Fascinating and entertaining, you can spend hours here!

✉ **Blaesstraat 51–53**
☎ **02–5121299**
🚌 **Bus 20, 21, 48**

La Boutique de Tintin

The Mecca for lovers of the great comic-strip hero Tintin! They really have everything in this shop: posters, doormats, coffee mugs, T-shirts, comic strips and numerous other Tintin items. Other Hergé heroes, such as Quick and Flupke, are also represented.

✉ **Rue de la Colline 13**
☎ **02–5145152**
🚇 **Centraal Station**

FNAC

Thanks to a special purchasing system, the FNAC (Fédération Nationale d'Achats des Cadres) can offer books and CDs about 10 percent cheaper than other shops. The Brussels branch has a very extensive selection of Dutch, French, English and German books. Something for everyone. The music department too has quite an impressive number of titles.

✉ **Rue Neuve City 2**
☎ **02–2092211**
🚇 **Rogier or De Brouckère**
🚌 **23, 52, 55, 56, 81**

Neuhaus

At Neuhas you will find chocolate in every possible shape and size: chocolate bars, truffles, chocolate with mocca and filled with cream. One of the house specialities is the Temptatio, chocolate with coffee and fresh cream. So, if you're trying to lose weight, avoid this shop at all cost!

✉ **Koninginnegalerij 25**
Neuhaus also has a branch at the Grote Markt 27
☎ **02–5126359**
🚇 **Beurs**
🚌 **23, 52, 55, 56, 81**

L'Objet du Désir

Fashionable leather bags, beautiful designer lamps, and other trendy interior design items.

✉ **Grote Zavel 21**
☎ **02–5124243**
🚇 **Naamse Poort, Louiza**

Rosebud

Brussels has a fair number of exquisite lingerie shops, including Rosebud. This shop situated just at the start of uptown Brussels shows what classic lingerie should look like.

✉ **Rue de Rollebeek 48**
☎ **02–5140851**
🚇 **Naamse Poort, Louiza**

Wittamer
The most famous chocolate shop in Brussels has been in business since 1911. This is *the* address for chocolate, hand-made speciality chocolates and cakes. The shop caused a sensation in spring 2000 when it displayed three life-size chocolate bunnies in the shop window, with long ears, short skirts and suspenders.

✉ **Grote Zavel**
☎ **02–5123742**
🚇 **Naamse Poort, Louiza**

Diest
Grigio
This is the shop for expensive swimwear, exclusive lingerie and comfortable nightwear from Dior to Marlies Dekkers.

✉ **Schaffensestraat 66**
☎ **013–335809**

Leuven
Gobelijn
Large collection of new comic strips and cartoons.

✉ **Mechelsestraat 35**
☎ **016–235586**

Het Pakjeshuis
Idiosyncratic gift shop with many original trinkets for interior design.

✉ **Mechelsestraat 30**
☎ **016–290911**

Your Lifestyle Shop
Interior decoration, crazy lamps, vases and display-cases. If you're looking for something new or unusual to cheer up your house, you will certainly find it here.

✉ **Dietsestraat 102**
☎ **016–291000**

Limburg

Hasselt
Chris & Chrisstyle
Two boutiques situated opposite each other with fashion from leading and lesser-known labels, including Hugo, Gigue and Pauline B.

Chris ✉ **Kapelstraat 22**
☎ **011–221248**
Chris & Chrisstyle
✉ **Kapelstraat 39**
☎ **011–221248**

Grigio (► 107, Diest Branch)
✉ **Onze-Lieve-Vrouwestraat 8**
☎ **011–223425**

ZNJ
Exclusive ladies' fashion of Belgian design label.

✉ **Kapelstraat 10**
☎ **011–220766**

Mar le Beau
This mansion looks like a perfumery, but offers products for the whole body. Inside you will find a health centre, beauty parlour and nail studio. *The* address for peelings, algae treatments and relaxing massage.

✉ **Bampslaan 13**
☎ **011–242909**

Quetin
Idiosyncratic collection of ladies' and men's shoes

✉ **Kapelstraat 31**
☎ **011–222241**

Belgian Pop Music
To lovers of English-language pop music, Belgium is becoming more and more interesting as a country. After the success of bands such as dEUS, Zita Swoon and K's Choice, there is a new batch of bands. You can listen to the latest CDs by Arid, Novastar or Laïs in a music shop.

Where to Take the Children

Steam Museum

The town of Maldegem, east of Bruges, is known for its steam museum. Three of the steam engines on display at the museum are still regularly used on the museum railway Maldegem–Eeklo. A ride in the beautiful antique carriages, with wooden seating and a bar carriage, not only takes you back in time, but also gives a pleasant introduction to green Meetjesland.
🖂 Stationsplein 8, Maldegem ☎ 050-716852

Antwerp

Magic World (Mini-Antwerp)

In Mini-Antwerp, the city is brought back to manageable proportions. Suddenly, the Steen and the Onze-Lieve-Vrouwe-Kathedraal are only footsteps away from each other. A fun way to get an idea of the most important buildings of the city and their location.
🖂 Cockerillkaai, Hangar 15
☎ 03–2370329
🚋 14, 23

Nationaal Scheepvaart-museum Het Steen

The museum highlights maritime history and life at sea. There are also a number of interesting models.
🖂 Steenplein 1
☎ 03–2320850
🕐 Daily 10–4:45. Closed Mon
🚌 Bus 6, 36

Pirateneiland

In this indoor play paradise, housed in an old warehouse, children will find a pirate ship, climbing ropes, ball ponds and an adventure trail with Tibetan bridges.
🖂 Kribbestraat 12
☎ 03–2315813
🕐 Wed 12–6, Thu–Fri 9:30–3:30, Sat–Sun, feast days and school holidays 10–6
🚋 4, 7

Rondvaart

A boat trip on the Scheldt offers children and adults the opportunity to see Antwerp and its harbour in an entertaining way. The mooring place of the Flandria shipping firm is within walking distance of the Grote Markt, on the Steenplein. Some tickets

allow you to combine a boat trip with a visit to the Zoo.
For more information:
☎ 03–2313100

Zoo

More than 4,000 animals, an Egyptian elephant temple, a massive aquarium and a sea otter and penguin sanctuary: you can easily spend a whole day here.
🖂 Koningin Astridplein 26
☎ 03–2024540
🕐 Open daily 9. Closing times vary according to the season
🚋 2, 3, 10, 11, 12, 15, 24; bus 16, 17, 18, 23, 27, 31, 32

Kalmthout

Suske and Wiske Kindermuseum

The Suske and Wiske children's museum is housed in the former residence of Willy Vandersteen, the spiritual father of Suske and Wiske. On the first floor, new Suske and Wiske comic books are signed, whilst on the ground floor, children can make their own comic strip in the workshop.
🖂 Beuvaislaan 98
☎ 03–6666485
🕐 by appointment for groups and during family days

Lichtaart
Bobbejaanland (▶ 40)

The Bobbejaanland family park in Lichtaart has more than 50 attractions for children and adults, including the Speedy Bob roller coaster, the Looping and the Whirlwind.
🖂 Olensesteenweg 45
☎ 014–557811 🕐 Days of opening vary each year (▶ 40)
Apr–Oct off-peak 10–5, and in high season 9:30–6:30

Mechelen
Dierenpark Planckendael
Planckendael is a large animal park, where the habitat of different animals resembles their natural one as closely as possible.

🖂 **Leuvensesteenweg 582, Muizen-Mechelen**
☎ **015–414921**

Speelgoedmuseum
An extensive collection of antique and new toys, including, of course, cowboys and Indians, dolls and model trains.

🖂 **Nekkerspoelstraat 21**
☎ **015–557075**
🕐 **Tue–Sun 10–5. Closed 1 Jan and 25 Dec**

West Flanders

Lustige Velodrome (➤ 48)
The Lustige Velodrome aims to make life as difficult as possible for cyclists. Every bicycle has a different quirk, which makes it almost impossible to cycle in a straight line.

🖂 **Next to the Blankenberge pier** ☎ **050–427020**
🕐 **Easter–15 Sep Mon–Sun 9–6**

Brussels
Atomium
Enormous museum in the shape of an iron molecule enlarged 165 billion times. The collection is somewhat sleep-inducing, but most children enjoy a visit to the building itself. The different spheres are interconnected by long escalators. From the highest sphere, the panorama is breathtaking.

🖂 **Eeuwfeestlaan**
☎ **02–4748977/02–4748904**
🚇 **Heizel**
🚌 **23, 81; bus 84, 89**

Centre Belge de la Bande Dessinée (Centrum voor het beeldverhaal ➤ 73)
More commonly known as the Stripmuseum, this comic-strip museum is ideal for children and adult fans of comic strips to visit together. Children will find a large number of their heroes immortalised in drawings and in 3D, while parents can see how well-known comic-strip artists have set about their work.

🖂 **Zandstraat 20**
☎ **02–2191980**
🚇 **Kruidtuin, Centraal Station of Rogier**
🚌 **23, 22, 55, 56, 81, 90, 92, 93, 94**

Mini Europe
From the Tower of Pisa to Big Ben: Mini Europe has brought together important buildings from all over Europe. This park, at the foot of the Atomium, contains some 300 scaled-down monuments, including the Grand-Place in Brussels, the Arena in Seville, the Houses of Parliament in London and the Doges' Palace in Venice.

🖂 **Voetballaan 1, Bruparck**
☎ **02–4741313**
🚇 **Heizel, Houba**
🚌 **23, 81; bus 84, 89**

Scientastic Museum
In this hands-on museum, children learn a number of principles of physics through carrying out simple experiments.

🖂 **Metrostation Beurs (level 1), Brussels**
☎ **02–7365335**
🕐 **Sat–Sun, feast days and school holidays 2–5:30**
🚇 **Beurs**
🚌 **23, 52, 55, 56, 81**

Manneken's Wardrobe
The Broodhuis in the Grand-Place in Brussels houses the museum of the city of Brussels. On the second floor is a display of all the costumes which Manneken Pis has worn on official occasions. You can admire the manneken as Dracula, samurai and pilot.

Museums

Comic-strip Route

As in Hasselt, many gables in the city centre of Brussels are painted with comic-strip figures. The comic strip route, available from the tourist office in Brussels, will lead you past 17 statues and comic-strip gables of Lucky Luke, Quick and Flupke, and Suske and Wiske, to name but a few. A fitting introduction to the comic-strip city of Brussels. Tourist office and information, Brussels:

✉ Hôtel de Ville, Grand Place
☎ 02-5138940

Antwerp
Nationaal Scheepvaart-museum

As a result of a Scheldt maritime exhibition held in 1925, many citizens of Antwerp expressed a desire to set up a maritime museum. This wish became reality in 1927 when the Stedelijk Scheepvaart-museum was founded and housed in a wing of the former Rijkshandelshoge-school.

✉ **Located in the former Rijkshandelshogeschool**

Bruges
Gruuthusemuseum

Housed in the 15th-century palace of the Heren van Gruuthuse, this museum undoubtedly has a very varied collection of applied art and decorative art from Bruges. You can also see a large collection of statues, tapestries and furniture, as well as silverware, copper tin, coins, medals, ceramics and musical instruments. The gun-room contains a notorious 18th-century guillotine.

✉ **Centre of Bruges**
☻ **1 Apr–30 Sep, open daily 9:30–5**

Leuven
Schatkamer van St Pieter

The Schatkamer van St Pieter is a museum of religious art, which also houses the world-famous triptych *The Last Supper* by Dirk Bouts. There are also many other paintings commissioned by the church, sculptures, church furniture and a collection of silverware.

✉ **Grote Markt**
☻ **Tue–Fri 10–5, Sat 10–4:30**

Stedelijk Museum Vander Kelen-Mertens

Applied art, including the historic salons of the 19th-century mansion, formerly Savoy College. Late-Gothic sculptures, paintings, porcelain, stained-glass windows and silverware. Archaeological department with objects excavated in Leuven and surroundings.

✉ **Savoyestraat 6**
☻ **Tue–Sat 10–5**

Museum de Spoelberg

This is a small, new museum, open only occasionally, with works of art from the de Spoelberg legacy: silverware, Chinese porcelain, and a collection of recently restored furniture and paintings from the 16th to the 19th century.

✉ **Naamsestraat 40**
☻ **Every second Sat of the month 2–5**

Tongeren
Gallo-Romeins Museum (► 89)

In the heart of Tongeren, on the site of what once was a large luxury Roman villa, now stands the Gallo-Romeins Museum (Gallo-Roman Museum). As an exhibition space for many local finds and as a symbol of the archaeological importance of the region, this museum is entirely bound up with the city, its history and its culture, which has been given an extra dimension. In this unique museum, designed according to the concept of a Roman city, the visitor is invited on a fascinating journey of discovery.

✉ **For more information contact: VVV Tongeren, Stadhuisplein 9**

Classical Music

Antwerp
Koninklijk Filharmonisch Orkest van Vlaanderen

The Koninklijk Filharmonisch Orkest van Vlaanderen (Royal Philharmonic Orchestra of Flanders) was founded in the mid-1950s and built up a solid reputation as an interpreter of the romantic repertoire. From 1985, the orchestra has also focused on 20th-century music. Philippe Herreweghe has been its musical director since September 1998 and international interest in the orchestra is increasing rapidly under his leadership. Herreweghe was responsible for a sensational Bruckner cycle. The orchestra also highlights recent Flemish composers, such as Luc Brewaes.

✉ **Braziliëstraat 15**
☎ **0800–21036 (reservations)**

Vlaamse Opera

The Vlaamse Opera (Flemish Opera) has grown into a leading institute for opera and music. In addition to well-known opera repertoire, such as the much-praised Puccini cycle, the programme regularly features lieder recitals.

✉ **Frankrijlei 3**
☎ **03–2336685** 🚇 **Leysstraat**

Mechelen
Carillon concerts

Mechelen is known for its carillon school. The St Romboutskathedraal hosts carillon concerts from 1 June to 15 September. One of the best places to listen to the concerts is the Minderbroedersgang, in front of the cathedral.

🕐 **Mon 8:30PM**

Brussels
Théâtre Royal de la Monnaie (Muntschouwburg)

This is the best-known opera theatre in Belgium. The striking, deep, bowl-shaped theatre was once the site of the riots which led to Belgium's independence. The individual programming and varied repertoire ensure that many performances are sold out well in advance. Try to book early.

✉ **Muntplein** ☎ **02–2291211**
Reservations: 02–2291200
🚇 **De Brouckère**

Palais des Beaux-Arts (Paleis voor de Schone Kunsten)

The Palace of Fine Arts was built by Victor Horta in 1928. Every year in May, this is the venue of the Koningin-Elisabethconcours, one of the most prestigious music competitions in Europe. A performance in the competition is often the start of a promising career. The categories include piano, violin, composition and song.

✉ **Ravesteinstraat 23**
☎ **02–5078220**
Information on the Elisabethconcours:
☎ **02–5130099**
🚇 **Centraal Station**

St Jan-en-Stefaan-der-Minimen-kerk

This baroque church close to the Marolles is one of the few places where the public can decide for themselves what to pay for a performance. Regular concerts and recitals of early music.

✉ **Minimenstraat 62**
☎ **02–5119384**
🚌 **Bus 48**

Puppet Theatre

Puppet and marionette theatre is very popular in Flanders. This certainly applies to the Antwerp Puppet Theatre – 'Poesje' for short – a marionette theatre where actual events and local celebrities are commented on in vivid Antwerp dialect. The texts are difficult to follow, even for Dutch-speaking people, but if you want to witness authentic popular entertainment, it is certainly worth a visit.

✉ Repenstraat (near the Vleeshuis)
Reservations through the Volkskundemuseum:
☎ **03–2329409**

Theatre & Film

Subtitling Films
Most foreign feature films shown in Flanders are subtitled in two languages – French and Dutch. Dubbed versions are sometimes shown but only in Brussels. The abbreviations in cinema programmes can help in choosing a film. *VO* means 'original version', and the abbreviation *V angl* indicates an English-language version.

Antwerp
Metropolis
The largest cinema complex in Antwerp is situated outside the centre of the city. The 24 screens all have the latest sound and projection systems, but it is the high-tech interior which speaks most to the imagination – a 21st-century cinema experience.

✉ **Groenendaallaan 394**
☎ **03–5443611/0900–00555**

deSingel
The international centre for the arts, Theater deSingel, highlights new developments in theatre, dance and serious music. The programming varies from Beethoven to Qawali Sufi songs, and from Jan Fabre to Teresa de Keersmaeker.

✉ **Desguinlei 25**
☎ **03–2483900**
🚋 **38**

Théâtre de Toone
If you'd like to see authentic Brussels marionette theatre then a visit to this puppet theatre for adults is a must. It was founded in 1830 by Antoine Genty, whose first name soon changed into the Flemish 'Toone'. Toone quickly built up a reputation for marionette performances of classical plays, such as *Macbeth* and *Faust*. Many performances are in Bruxelois, the Brussels dialect, a curious (and sometimes incomprehensible) mixture of French and Flemish. There is also a museum where you can look at an exhibition of puppets in the interval.

✉ **Schuddeveldgang 6**
☎ **02–5117137** 🎟 ☎ **Closed Sun** 🚈 **Centraal Station**

Brussels
Kinepolis
In the Heizel district stands one of the largest cinema complexes in the country. Kinepolis has 26 screens, including an Imax theatre with a giant 600sq m screen. Most English-language films will be subtitled, but check to make sure it is not dubbed (see marginal note).

✉ **Eeuwfeestlaan 1, Bruparck**
☎ **Reservations: 02–4742604,**
🚇 **Heizel**

Ghent
Arca
Arca is the oldest fringe theatre in Flanders. The theatre is in a warehouse by the River Lieve, and has a reputation for experimental and avant-garde pieces. Arca regularly offers space to new Flemish playwrights. The Tinnenpotheater now also stages performances, especially cabaret.

✉ **St Widostraat 4**
✉ **Tinnenpotstraat 21**
☎ **09–2251860**
🚋 **Gravensteen 1, 10, 11, 12, 13;**
bus: Korenmarkt, 3, 38

Vooruit Arts Centre
In the 1980s, the former social hall of the Socialist Cooperative Vooruit was saved from demolition and converted into a flourishing centre for the arts. The programming includes theatre (from Judith Herzberg to Samuel Beckett), music (from Benjamin Britten to Misha Mengelberg) and dance. There are regular disco evenings in the ballroom.

✉ **St Pietersnieuwstraat 23**
☎ **09–2672828**
🚋 **Bagattenstraat 1, 10, 11, 12;**
bus: St Pietersnieuwstraat 5, 6, 50

Jazz, Pop & Nightclubs

Antwerp

Café d'Anvers

In the middle of the red-light district of Antwerp is Café d'Anvers, a popular disco where new trends in dancing alternate with the old familiar disco beats. The disco, which is housed in a former cinema, regularly invites well-known DJs.

- ✉ Verversrui 15
- ☎ 03–2263870
- 🕐 Fri–Sat 11PM–7:30AM
- 🚌 Bus 6, 34

Sportpaleis

As the name indicates, the Sportpaleis in Antwerp was originally set up for sporting events, such as the four-day cycle racing events. These days, 'De Oude Dame' (the old lady), as the residents of Antwerp call the place, is used for large-scale events such as 'the night of the proms', shows, revues and concerts by stars such as Whitney Houston.

- ✉ Schijnpoortweg 113
- ☎ 070–345345
- 🚇 Schijnpoort

Zillion

This mega discotheque, in the Antwerp district Het Zuid, is the Valhalla for house and techno-loving Flanders. Within the walls of a former sports hall and a squash complex are now four different discos, each with its own atmosphere and musical style. Zillion offers a platform for the latest trends, supported by much technical gadgetry, enormous light batteries, and a robot which sometimes dances along.

- ✉ Jan van Ghentstraat 4
- ☎ 03–2481516 🕐 Thu–Sun from 10PM 🚌 6

Bruges

Cactus Club

The popular Cactus Club highlights new developments in pop, jazz and world music, but also regularly makes room for nostalgic events, such as rock 'n' roll and sixties evenings.

- ✉ St Jacobsstraat 33
- ☎ 050–331014
- 🚌 Bus 3, 13

Brussels

Le Bazaar

Small club in the Brussels working-class district, the Marolles. Upstairs is a dimly lit restaurant, downstairs you can dance to soul, funk and rock music.

- ✉ Rue des Capucins 63
- 🚇 Munthof

Fuse

Fuse is the first techno club to open its doors in Belgium. Renowned DJs such as Dave Clarke, Laurent Garnier and 100% Isis play their music here, and Björk once performed at Fuse. *The address for party animals and dance fanatics with stamina. There is a gay party every Saturday night under the name *La Demence.*

- ✉ Blaesstraat 208
- ☎ 02–511 97 89
- 🕐 Sat 10PM–7AM (entrance free until 11PM)

Ghent

Damberd

The Damberd in Ghent has a rich history: the building has been continuously used as a café since the 15th century. Since 1978, Damberd has presented itself as an intercultural jazz café.

- ✉ Korenmarkt 19
- ☎ 09–329 53 37

Carnival

Although the Walloon carnivals (especially those in Binche, Eupen and Stavelot) are the better-known, Flemish people are also formidable carnival-goers. The festivities take place between January and April, and often involve parades and a funfair at the Grote Markt. The best-known carnivals are those in Ostend and Aalst. In Aalst, the *Ajuinen worp* (throwing of onions) takes place on the Monday. The following day, the festival reaches its peak during the dance of the Voil Jeannetten, a group of brightly dressed transvestites.

- ☎ 053–732230 🕐 Sun, Mon and Shrove Tuesday

Miscellaneous

Casinos

Belgium has eight casinos which are open all year. Four of these are situated on the Flemish coast; in Blankenberge, Knokke, Middelkerke and Ostend. In general, the casinos also play an important cultural role. The gambling palaces are also used as conference and exhibition spaces, theatres and concert halls. The Ostend casino has the best reputation. The famous conductor Herbert von Karajan was even of the opinion that this hall has the best acoustics in the world.

Botanique

The Botanique is now the seat of the French-speaking community in Brussels. The building dates from 1826 and was erected in neo-classical style. Part of the botanical gardens which belong to it had to make way for the building of the north–south link. The remaining area of the herb garden was converted into a cultural centre in 1984. The enormous conservatories, which house a theatre, a cinema and an exhibition space, are regular venues for music events, such as the Festival de la Chanson, which takes place every September. The large Orangery is a popular place for staging rock concerts.

✉ **Koningsstraat 236, Brussels**
☎ **02–2261211**
🚇 **Botanique/Kruidtuin**
🚌 **Bus 38, 61, 92, 94**

Casino Blankenberge

The Casino Blankeberge not only has gambling rooms, but also houses an art gallery, bar, tavern and restaurant. There is also ample parking for patrons only.

✉ **Zeedijk 150, Blankenberge**
☎ **050–419840**
🕐 **Gambling room: Mon–Sun 3PM–6AM**

Wellington Racecourse

Gamblers and horse-racing enthusiasts can enjoy the summer months at the atmospheric Wellington Racecourse in Ostend, a remnant of the 19th century. The racecourse has two tracks: a lava track for trotting and a grass track for galloping.

✉ **Hippodroom Wellington, Koningin Astridlaan, Ostend**
☎ **059–806055** 🕐 **15 Jun– 15 Sep: Fri evening trotting, Sat–Sun galloping**

Casino van Knokke

The Knokke Casino is one of the haunts of the international beau monde. At the gambling tables for roulette, black jack and poker you can place your bet well into the early hours of the morning. You can also admire the splendid interior, which includes works by Magritte, Delveaux and Keith Haring. The monumental chandelier of Venetian glass is apparently the largest in the world.

✉ **Zeedijk Albertstrand 507, Knokke** ☎ **050–630505**

Ghent Floraliën

Every five years, Ghent justifies its name as a city of flowers during the *Floraliën*, a large-scale show of house and garden plants, and many flowers. Since 2000, there have also been themed gardens on display.

✉ **Flanders Expo, St Denijs Westrem, Ghent**
☎ **09–2419211 or 09–2415099**
🕐 **Every five years in the last week of Apr. Next show 2005**

Sinksenfoor

During the six weeks after Whitsun, the open space between the Vlaamse and Waalse quays are filled with a mega funfair, which the residents of Antwerp call the Sinksenfoor. This fair, whose huge ferris wheel is visible from afar, offers an endless range of attractions, from shooting galleries to a pirate ship and ghost house.

✉ **Between Vlaamse and Waalse Kaai, Antwerp**
🕓 **Six weeks following Whitsun**

Ghentse Feesten

The Ghent town festival has grown into a large-scale series of events, which draw millions of visitors every year. This ten-day programme of street events guarantees a series of mime, music and theatre performances, parades, barbecues and fireworks. On the Friday, the historical procession of the guild of noose bearers takes place. The starting signal for the festivities is given by the legendary Belleman on the Sunday closest to 22 July.

☎ **Information 09–2394260**

Carpet of Flowers on the Grand-Place (Brussels)

Every two years, the Grand-Place (Grote Markt) in Brussels is covered by an immense carpet of flowers, consisting of some 750 000 begonias. This flower carpet is a colourful sight, especially on a sunny day. It also highlights the size of this 100m-long and 68m-wide city square.

✉ **Grote Markt, Brussels**
🕓 **14–16 Aug, in even-numbered years**

Vierdaagse van de IJzer

At the end of August, the four-day international walking event in remembrance of World War I takes place in the Westhoek. The walk, which consists of four loops of 32km (19 miles) each, runs across the IJzervlakte and past the former trenches. Walkers can start in Diksmuide, Ieper, Poperinge or Oostduinkerke.

☎ **058–233305** 🕓 **Wed–Sat in the first full week after 15 Aug**

Cultuurmarkt van Vlaanderen

During the last weekend of August, the culture market of Flanders takes place in Antwerp. The dozens of mainly short performances give the public a taster of the music, theatre and dance performances coming up in the new season.

☎ **03–2320103 or 03–2330570**

Bokrijk Open-air Museum

Bokrijk is a large open-air museum devoted to reconstructed buildings and displays of different parts of Flanders. The museum grounds have, for example, villages from the Kempen and the Haspengouw, as well as a reconstruction of part of the old Antwerp city centre. Children can take part in various activities such as minigolf, clog-making and archery. In the popular sports tent they can also learn about Flemish national sports such as *beugelen* and *krulbollen*.

✉ **Domein Bokrijk, Genk, E314-exit Park Midden Limburg**
☎ **011–265300**

Stroppendragers

The procession of the *stroppendragers* (noose-bearers) dates from the time of Emperor Charles V. The emperor was regularly in conflict with the dignitaries of the city, who refused to meet their tax obligations. Eventually, Charles V came to Ghent in person and gave orders to have the ramparts demolished. He decided not to destroy the city of his birth any further. Instead, he forced the dignitaries to walk through the city barefoot and with nooses round their necks. To this day, the city celebrates the event as a moral victory.

🕓 During the Ghent Festival in July

What's On When

Ronde van Vlaanderen Cycle Race

This tour of Flanders is the most important sporting event of the province. The legendary cycle race, which starts in Bruges and finishes in Meerbeke, leads through the Flemish Ardennes. The end of the race often takes place on the *muur* ('wall') of Geraardsbergen, one of the few remaining sections of cobbled street in the race. Cyclists also have to tackle the climb up the Kluisberg, the Oude Kwaremont and the Bosberg.
☎ Information on the *muur* of Geraardsbergen: VVV Geraardsbergen 054–437289
⏱ Mar–Apr; depending on the cycle-racing calendar of the relevant year

Giants

Many folkloristic processions and parades in Flanders include giants. The giants emerged in many cities at the end of the Middle Ages and probably originate from a procession in which the story of David and Goliath was acted out. Well-known giants include Polydor, Polydra and Klein Polysorke in Aalst, and Pie, Wanneke and Jomme in Tervuren.

January
Procession and Pretzel-Throwing (Garaadsbergen)

Once a year, prominent citizens of Geraardsbergen are allowed to bombard 'the common folk' with pretzels (*krakelingen*). First, however, they have to drink wine from a goblet containing live fish. The fish have to be swallowed alive. The throwing of the pretzels is preceded by a folkloristic procession in which all figures from the history of Geraardsbergen are represented.
✉ Oudenberg Geraardsbergen
⏱ Last Sun in Feb

March
Het Bal van de Dode Rat (Dead Rat's Ball) (Ostend)

This big charity ball, which has a different theme each year, is one of the highlights of the Ostend carnival. Participants have to dress up and wear masks. The painter James Ensor was one of the initiators of the ball, which owes its name to the cabaret *Le Rat Mort* in Paris.
✉ Kursaal Casino, Ostend
☎ 059–705111 or 059–701199
⏱ First Sat in Mar

May
Kattenstoet (Cats' Parade), Ieper (Ypres)

The Kattenstoet in Ieper is one of the best-known folkloristic parades in Flanders. In former times, the residents of Ieper used to throw live cats from the belfry to conclude the annual market. This ritual was seen as a challenge to the devil. The cats' parade, which developed later, is headed by the giant cats Cieper and Minneke Poes. The cats which are thrown from the belfry nowadays are the soft-toy variety.
☎ 057-228584 ⏱ Once every three years on the second Sun in May; the next one takes place in 2003

May–June
Heilig-Bloedprocessie (Holy Blood Procession) (Bruges)

The Heilig-Bloedprocessie in Bruges is the best-known procession in Flanders. During this religious procession, the relic of the Holy Blood – a tube supposed to contain some drops of Christ's blood– is carried through the streets of Bruges. The relic has been preserved in the Basilica of the Holy Blood for years; it is alleged that the blood became fluid for a while every Friday. The procession, in which many important clergymen take part, is enhanced by groups wearing costumes which portray scenes from the Old and New Testaments.
⏱ Hemelvaart

August–September
Reuzenomgang (Giants' Procession), Dendermonde

Every year in Dendermonde, there is a parade with three guild giants. During this procession, the giants 'Goliath', 'Indiaan' and 'Mars' are surrounded by more than 600 participants in medieval costume. This colourful event draws huge crowds of visitors to the city every year.
☎ 052–213956 ⏱ Thu after the fourth Sun in Aug

Practical Matters

Above: *Kriek, Gueuze and Faro beer: matured in oak barrels*
Below: *the Brussels metro*

TIME DIFFERENCES

GMT	Belgium	British Summer	Netherlands	USA (NY)	USA (LA)
12 noon →	1PM	1PM →	1PM →	7AM ←	4AM →

BEFORE YOU GO

WHAT YOU NEED

- ● Required
- ○ Suggested
- ▲ Not required

	Belgium	Netherlands	Germany	UK	USA
Passport/National Identity Card	●	●	●	●	●
Visa	▲	▲	▲	▲	▲
Onward or Return Ticket	▲	○	○	○	○
Health Inoculations	▲	▲	▲	▲	▲
Health Documentation (► Health, 123)	▲	●	●	●	●
Travel Insurance	○	○	○	○	○
Driving Licence (national)	●	●	●	●	●
Green Card (if own car)	▲	●	●	●	●
Car Registration Document (if own car)	▲	●	●	●	●

WHEN TO GO

Flanders

 High season

☐ Low season

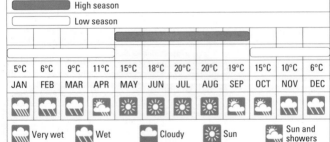

5°C	6°C	9°C	11°C	15°C	18°C	20°C	20°C	19°C	15°C	10°C	6°C
JAN	FEB	MAR	APR	MAY	JUN	JUL	AUG	SEP	OCT	NOV	DEC

Very wet · Wet · Cloudy · Sun · Sun and showers

TOURIST OFFICES

In the UK
Belgian Tourist Office
29 Princes Street
London W1R 7RG
☎ 0900–1887799

In the USA
Suite 1501
780 Third Avenue
New York NY 10017
☎ 212–7588130

In Belgium
Toerisme Vlaanderen
Grasmarkt 63
1000 Brussels
☎ 02–5040390

POLICE 101

FIRE 100

AMBULANCE 100

WHEN YOU ARE THERE

ARRIVING

There are charter flights and scheduled flights from all important European airports to the national airport of Zaventem, some 14km (8.5 miles) northeast of Brussels. ☎ 02–7533913 for flight information. The Belgian airline Sabena maintains frequent flight routes to all parts of the world. Many budget and charter airlines also fly to cities in the region.

Flanders is also accessible by train or car. British visitors can take Eurostar to Brussels Midi station and from there to Ghent, Bruges, Antwerp or other major cities. Alternatively, there are regular ferries to the ports of Ostend and Zeebrugge.

Zaventem Airport Distance to city centre	**Journey times**
25km (16 miles)	🚆 30 minutes
	🚌 35 minutes
	🚗 20 minutes

MONEY

The unit of currency is the euro but until December 2001, the Belgian franc will continue to be used. A dual pricing system will operate. In January 2002 euro bank notes and coins will replace the Belgian franc which will cease to be legal tender in July 2002. Euro notes come in denominations of 10, 20, 50, 100, 200 and 500 and coins in denominations of 1, 2, 5, 10, 20 and 50 centimes, 1 and 2 euros.

TIME

 Belgium follows Central European Time (CET) which is one hour ahead of Greenwich Mean Time (GMT+1), but from the end of March to the end of October it is on summertime (GMT+2).

CUSTOMS

 YES

From a non-EU country for personal use:
Cigarettes: 200 or
Tobacco: 250 grams
Spirits : 1 litre or
Fortified wine (sherry, port): 2 litres
Wine: 2 litres

From an EU country for personal use (guidelines):
Cigarettes: 800 or
Tobacco: 1 kilogram
Spirits: 10 litres or
Fortified wine: 20 litres
Wine: 90 litres
Beer: 110 litres

 NO

Drugs, firearms, explosives, offensive weapons, protected animal species.

EMBASSIES

UK
02–2876211

USA
02–5082111

Australia
02–2310500

Canada
02–7410611

WHEN YOU ARE THERE

TOURIST OFFICES

Toerisme Vlaanderen
● Grasmarkt 61
 1000 Brussels
 ☎ 02–5040396

**Provincial VVVs
(Tourist Offices)
Province of Antwerp**
● Koningin Elisabethlei 16
 2018 Antwerp
 ☎ 03–2406373

West Flanders
● Kasteel Tillegem
 8200 Bruges
 ☎ 050–380296

East Flanders
● P.A.C. Het Zuid
 Woodrow Wilsonplein 3
 9000 Ghent
 ☎ 09–2677020

Flemish Brabant
● Diestsesteenweg 52
 3010 Leuven
 ☎ 016–267620

Limburg
● Universiteitslaan 1
 Hasselt ☎ 011–237450

**Local offices
Antwerp**
● Grote Markt 15
 2000 Antwerp
 ☎ 03–2320103

Bruges
● Burg 11
 8000 Bruges
 ☎ 050–448686

Ghent
● Botermarkt 17a
 9000 Ghent
 ☎ 09–2665232

Brussels
● Grand-Place
 1000 Brussels
 ☎ 02–5138940

NATIONAL HOLIDAYS

J	F	M	A	M	J	J	A	S	O	N	D
1		(1)	(1)	1(2)	(2)	2	1	1		2	1

1 Jan	New Year's Day
Mar/Apr	Easter Monday
1 May	May Day
May/Jun	Ascension Day
May/Jun	Whit Monday
11 Jul	Flemish National Day
21 Jul	Belgian National Day
15 Aug	Assumption
27 Sep	Walloon National Day
1 Nov	All Saints' Day
11 Nov	Armistice Day
25 Dec	Christmas Day

Most shops, banks and offices are closed on these days. The Flemish and Walloon National Days are not official holidays but they are generally celebrated.

OPENING TIMES

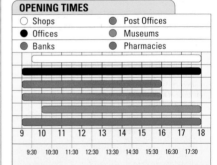

○ Shops	● Post Offices
● Offices	● Museums
● Banks	● Pharmacies

Some shops close in the afternoon. Other shops are open on Saturday but closed on Monday. In major cities you will find a number of shops that are open beyond normal hours until 1 or 2AM or even all night. Pharmacies have a night and weekend rota which is displayed on the door of all pharmacies when they are closed. You can also ask the tourist office for details of the duty pharmacist.

The opening times for museums vary enormously, ask at the individual museum or at the tourist office. Most are closed on Monday.

DRIVE ON THE RIGHT

TOILETS NOT FREE

PUBLIC TRANSPORT

Trains The Belgian railway network is one of the densest in Europe. The distances in Flanders are relatively small. Important cities such as Brussels, Antwerp, Ghent and Bruges are approximately one hour's distance from each other. Most of the larger cities also have frequent railway links, so you never need to wait very long for a connection.

Tickets are bought in advance at the ticket office. The Belgian Railways (NMBS) offer discounts on weekend tickets and tickets for more than one day's travel. It is possible to take a bicycle on an inland journey for a small extra charge.

Buses Most links between smaller towns and villages are by bus. The buses generally drive back and forth between different NMBS stations. Tickets for a single journey or a day pass may be bought from the driver. Cheaper tickets for ten journeys are available from the offices of De Lijn.

Trams and Metro Trams operate in most of the larger cities. Brussels has an extensive underground train network, which is especially handy for greater distances: stations are indicated with a large white or yellow M (for metro). In Antwerp there are a number of so-called pre-metro lines. These refers to trams which cover part of their route underground.

The coastal tram, which covers the 67km (41 miles) along the Flemish coast several times a day is a very handy and attractive form of transport. With a tram ticket you can also get discounts for entry to some tourist attractions.

CAR RENTAL

All major car hire firms have offices in Flanders. They usually state as one of their conditions for hiring a car that the driver should be over 21 years of age (in some cases even 25).

TAXIS

Taxis can be hailed in the street. The charge is dependent on the number of kilometres. For longer journeys, it is sometimes wiser to agree a charge with the driver in advance. The tip is included in the charge.

DRIVING

Speed limit on motorways and roads with separate lanes and dual carriageways: **120 kmph**

Speed limit on dual carriageways with lanes separated by one white line, and other roads: **90 kmph**

Speed limit in built-up areas: **50 kmph**

Front and rear seat belts are mandatory.

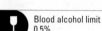

Blood alcohol limit 0.5%. Random breath tests are made regularly.

Petrol is sold by the litre in Belgium. Filling stations have standard 98 octane unleaded petrol, 95 octane unleaded petrol, lead-substitute and diesel. Most filling stations are self-service and accept credit cards.

Many car rental firms in Flanders have their own breakdown and/or emergency number. On motorways you can use the SOS phones of the Touring Wegenhulp or Touring Secours. In the event of a breakdown on other roads you can call the central number 24 hours a day.

PERSONAL SAFETY

In general, Flanders is a safe area in which to travel, but in the big cities there are some districts which are better avoided after midnight. There are regular pickpockets on the underground trains in Brussels. If you become a victim of theft, contact the police as soon as possible. Remember to ask for a signed report, which you will need to recover any loss from your insurance company. Do not leave valuables in the back of your car and use the hotel safe, if possible.

Police assistance:
☎ **101**

TELEPHONES

For most public telephones in Flanders you now need a (pre-paid) phone card. You can buy them from any post-office, kiosk and from some supermarkets. The country code for Belgium is 00–32. When you call

Belgium from outside the country, you need to omit the first 0 of the area code. You then dial a seven-digit (Brussels, Antwerp and Ghent) or six-digit number.

International Dialling Codes

From Belgium to:	
UK:	**00 44**
Ireland:	**00 353**
USA/Canada:	**00 1**
Netherlands:	**00 31**
Australia:	**00 61**

POST

Stamps can be bought at the post-office or from a machine. Letters weighing less than 20g have a fixed rate within the EU; the weight and measurements of the envelope determine the price for destinations outside the EU. Most post offices are open daily from 9AM to 5PM.

ELECTRICITY

In Belgium the power supply is 220 volts. Plugs are round with two pins. British

appliances will need an adaptor. For most non-European equipment you will also need a transformer to 100–120 volts AC.

TIPS/GRATUITIES

Yes ✓ No ✗		
Restaurants	✗	
Hotels (chambermaids, porters)	✗	
Bars	✗	
Doormen in discos	✓	
Taxis	✗	
Guides	✓	
Cloakroom attendants	✓	
Toilets	✓	
Hairdressers	✓	

PHOTOGRAPHY

What to photograph: medieval gables and alleyways, guild houses, churches and belfries. In the majority of places, most historic buildings are found around the Grote Markt (main square).

Best time to take photographs: in the summer before 11AM and in the afternoon after 4PM. At the beginning and end of the day, the colours are usually more saturated.

Film and developing: at photo shops, kiosks and some stations.

HEALTH

Insurance
The costs of medical emergency treatment usually have to be paid on the spot. With an E111 form, EU citizens can often reclaim these costs in Belgium. Check your policy as to your rights and duties in the event of medical problems abroad.

Dental Services
In the event of unexpected toothache or other dental problems, it is best to contact the nearest dentist. Most hotel receptionists can help to find a suitable dentist. Make sure that your medical insurance covers dental treatment.

Sun Advice
Sunshine in Flanders usually brings about a nice bustle on the terraces and beaches. Some days, however, the sun can be deceptively fierce and a bout of sunbathing can have unpleasant consequences. This certainly applies to people who are sensitive to the sun, so it is best to be careful and limit your sunbathing.

Drugs
Belgian pharmacies have many medicines available. Nevertheless, it is handy to take a supply of the medicines which you regularly need. It is also advisable to take a leaflet or list of active components, so that the pharmacy can find an alternative under a different product name, if necessary.

Safe Water
It is safe to drink tap water anywhere in Flanders, but sometimes bottled water may taste better. Flemish café-restaurants usually offer still or sparkling mineral water.

CONCESSIONS

Most museums in Flanders offer reduced entrance fees for children. Children under five are usually free. Students regularly receive discounts on entrance fees: discount conditions and percentages, however, vary from one museum to another.

In addition, there are a number of concessions for senior citizens, visitors with disabilities and groups.

CLOTHING SIZES

UK	USA	Belgium /Europe	
36	36	46	
38	38	48	
40	40	50	
42	42	52	Suits
44	44	54	
46	46	56	
7	8	41	
7.5	8.5	42	
8.5	9.5	43	
9.5	10.5	44	Shoes
10.5	11.5	45	
11	12	46	
14.5	14.5	37	
15	15	38	
15.5	15.5	39/40	
16	16	41	Shirts
16.5	16.5	42	
17	17	43	
8	6	34	
10	8	36	
12	10	38	
14	12	40	Dresses
16	14	42	
18	16	44	
4.5	6	38	
5	6.5	38	
5.5	7	39	
6	7.5	39	Shoes
6.5	8	40	
7	8.5	41	

123

WHEN DEPARTING

- If you are checking in from Brussels on an intercontinental flight, you normally need to arrive at the airport two hours in advance. For flights within Europe, the check-in time varies from one hour to an hour and a half. Ask your airline or travel agent well in advance.

LANGUAGE

The state of Belgium, of which Flanders forms a part, has been divided by a language barrier ever since its inception in 1830. Dutch is spoken north of the linguistic divide, whilst French is the language of communication south of the language border. The Dutch-speaking area roughly falls into the territory of the district of Flanders. The only exception is the 'metropolitan district' of Brussels. Brussels is officially bilingual, but in practice some 80 percent of the Brussels population uses French. Most Flemish people also have a reasonable command of English, French and German, especially in touristic areas.

hotel	*hotel*	breakfast	*ontbijt*
room	*kamer*	toilet	*toilet/WC*
single/	*eenpersoonskamer/*	bathroom	*badkamer*
double	*tweepersoonskamer*	shower	*douche*
one/two nights	*een/twee nachten*	balcony	*balkon*
per person/	*per persoon/*	key	*sleutel*
per room	*per kamer*	room service	*room service*
reservation	*reservering*	chambermaid	*kamermeisje*
rate	*prijs*		

bank	*bank*	American dollar	*Amerikaanse dollar*
exchange office	*wisselkantoor*	banknote	*papiergeld*
post office	*postkantoor*	coin	*wisselgeld/kleingeld*
cashier	*kassa*	credit card	*creditcard*
foreign exchange	*buitenlands geld*	traveller's cheque	*reisecheque*
currency	*valuta*	exchange rate	*wisselkoers*
British pound	*Engels/Britse pond*	commission charge	*commissie*

restaurant	*restaurant*	starter	*voorgerecht*
café	*café*	main course	*hoofdgerecht*
table	*tafel*	dish of the day	*dagschotel*
menu	*menukaart*	dessert	*nagerecht*
set menu	*menu*	drink	*drank/drankje*
wine list	*wijnkaart*	waiter	*ober*
lunch	*lunch/middageten*	waitress	*serveerster*
dinner	*diner/avondeten*	the bill	*de rekening*

aeroplane	*vliegtuig*	single/return	*enkele reis/retour*
airport	*luchthaven*	first/	*eerste klas/*
train	*trein*	second class	*tweede klas*
station	*station*	ticket office	*boekingskantoor*
bus	*bus*	timetable	*dienstregeling*
station	*busstation*	seat	*plaats*
ferry	*veerboot*	non-smoking	*niet roken*
port	*haven*	reserved	*gereserveerd*
ticket	*reisekaart*	taxi!	*taxi!*

yes	*ja*	help!	*help!*
no	*nee*	today	*vandaag*
please	*alstublieft*	tomorrow	*morgen*
thank you	*dank u*	yesterday	*gisteren*
hello	*dag/hallo*	how much?	*hoeveel?*
goodbye	*dag/tot ziens*	expensive	*duur*
goodnight	*welterusten*	closed	*gesloten*
sorry	*excuseer/pardon*	open	*geopend*

INDEX

Acknowledgements
The publishers would like to thank the following photographers and libraries for their assistance in the preparation of this book:

James Ensor, zelfportret met maskers, 2000 c/o BEELDRECHT AMSTERDAM 14, BELGACOM 122, DIENST VOOR TOERISME BRUGGE 11, 45, DIENST VOOR TOERISME DAMME 49, DIENST VOOR TOERISME DENDERMONDE 58, 65, DIENST VOOR TOERISME DIKSMUIDE 16, 43, 57a, 57b, DIENST VOOR TOERISME HASSELT 86, DIENST VOOR TOERISME HOOGSTRA-TEN 39, DIENST VOOR TOERISME KORTRIJK 52, DIENST VOOR TOERISME MAASEIK 87a, DIENST VOOR TOERISME & CULTUUR NIEUWPOORT 10b, DIENST VOOR TOERISME ST.-TRUIDEN 88, JEROEN VAN DER SPEK 5a, 5b, 8a, 9a, 10a, 21, 23, 24, 27b, 35, 36, 38, 56, 60b, 62, 67, TEO VAN GERWEN DESIGN 9b, 63, TOERISME ANTWERPEN 1, 22, 37 TOERISME HASPENGOUW 18, TOERISME VLAANDEREN: A KOUPRIANOFF 15a, 15b, 31, 42, 91b, 117a, B ALLEGAERT 85, BRUSSELS GEWEST 17, 75b, 77, CARRASCO 72, C. POTIGNY 20, 51, D. DE KIEVITH 6, 8b, 28, 41, 44, 47, 53, 71, 76, 79, 91a, FOTOGRAFISCH ATELIER 55, 83, FREELANCE PICTURES 117b, GWAPO 60a, H.L. WEICHSELBAUM 27a, 70, 87b, 89, J. JACOBS 13, MICHALSKI 61, M. DECLEER 82, M. JOYE 19, P. POTIGNY 2, P. SMIT 7 SCHRAFRANSKI 73, TOERISME PROVINCIE ANTWERPEN 32, 40, TOERISME VLAANDEREN 26, 33, 46, 54, 59, 90, W. ROBBERECHTS 75a, W. SIEMOENS 12, 25, 66, 78 VVV BLANKENBERGE 48

Dear Essential Traveller

Your comments, opinions and recommendations are very important to us. So please help us to improve our travel guides by taking a few minutes to complete this simple questionnaire.

You do not need a stamp (unless posted outside the UK). If you do not want to cut this page from your guide, then photocopy it or write your answers on a plain sheet of paper.

Send to: **The Editor, AA World Travel Guides, FREEPOST SCE 4598, Basingstoke RG21 4GY.**

Your recommendations...

We always encourage readers' recommendations for restaurants, nightlife or shopping – if your recommendation is used in the next edition of the guide, we will send you a **_FREE_ AA _Essential_ Guide** of your choice. Please state below the establishment name, location and your reasons for recommending it.

_____
_____
_____
_____

Please send me **AA _Essential_** _____
(*see list of titles inside the front cover*)

About this guide...

Which title did you buy?
   AA _Essential_ _____
Where did you buy it? _____
When? <u>m m</u> / <u>y y</u>

Why did you choose an AA _Essential_ Guide? _____
_____
_____
_____
_____

Did this guide meet your expectations?
   Exceeded ☐ Met all ☐ Met most ☐ Fell below ☐
   Please give your reasons _____
_____
_____
_____

continued on next page...

Were there any aspects of this guide that you particularly liked? _____
_____
_____
_____

Is there anything we could have done better? _____
_____
_____
_____
_____

About you...

Name (*Mr/Mrs/Ms*) _____

Address _____

_____

_____ Postcode _____

Daytime tel nos _____

Which age group are you in?
Under 25 ☐ 25–34 ☐ 35–44 ☐ 45–54 ☐ 55–64 ☐ 65+ ☐

How many trips do you make a year?
Less than one ☐ One ☐ Two ☐ Three or more ☐

Are you an AA member? Yes ☐ No ☐

About your trip...

When did you book? m m / y y   When did you travel? m m / y y

How long did you stay? _____

Was it for business or leisure? _____

Did you buy any other travel guides for your trip?

If yes, which ones? _____

_____

Thank you for taking the time to complete this questionnaire. Please send
it to us as soon as possible, and remember, you do not need a stamp
(*unless posted outside the UK*).

Happy Holidays!